D0110265

THE MEANING IS
IN THE WAITING

PAULA GOODER

THE **MEANING** IS
IN THE **WAITING**

the spirit of advent

foreword by
LAUREN F. WINNER

PARACLETE PRESS
BREWSTER, MASSACHUSETTS

The Meaning Is in the Waiting: The Spirit of Advent

2013 Second Printing
2009 First Printing

Copyright © 2008 by Paula Gooder

ISBN: 978-1-55725-662-1

Library of Congress Cataloging-in-Publication Data
Gooder, Paula.
 The meaning is in the waiting : the spirit of Advent / Paula Gooder.
  p. cm.
 Originally published: Norwich : Canterbury Press, 2008.
 ISBN 978-1-55725-662-1
 1. Expectation (Psychology)—Religious aspects—Christianity. 2. Patience-
Religious aspects—Christianity. 3. Bible--Biography. 4. Advent. I. Title.
 BV4647.E93G66 2009
 242'.332—dc22   2009030989

First published in 2008 by the Canterbury Press, Norwich (a publishing
imprint of Hymns Ancient & Modern Limited, a registered charity), 13–17
Long Lane, London EC1A 9PN, www.scm-canterburypress.co.uk.

The author has asserted her right under the Copyright, Designs, and Patents
Act, 1988, to be identified as the "author of this work."

Unless otherwise indicated, Scripture quotations are from the New Revised
Standard Version of the Bible, copyright 1989, 1995 by the Division of
Christian Education of the National Council of the Churches of Christ in the
United States of America and are used by permission. All rights reserved.

Scripture verses referenced with NIV are taken from the HOLY BIBLE, NEW
INTERNATIONAL VERSION® NIV®. Copyright © 1973, 1978, 1984
by Biblica, Inc.™ Used by permission of Zondervan. All rights reserved
worldwide.

10 9 8 7 6 5 4 3 2

All rights reserved. No part of this book may be reproduced, stored in an
electronic retrieval system, or transmitted in any form or by any means—
electronic, mechanical, photocopy, recording, or any other—except for
brief quotations in printed reviews, without the prior permission of the
publisher.

Published by Paraclete Press
Brewster, Massachusetts
www.paracletepress.com
Printed in the United States of America

For Martin and Carol Gooder,
my father and mother in life as well as in faith,
with love

CONTENTS

FOREWORD   ix

HOW TO USE THIS BOOK   xiii

INTRODUCTION   3
A REFLECTION ON WAITING

ONE CALLED TO WAIT   23
     Abraham and Sarah,
     Our Ancestors in the Faith

TWO WAITING FOR THE DAY OF THE LORD   53
     The Prophets

THREE WAITING BETWEEN THE TIMES   83
       John the Baptist

FOUR A LIFETIME OF WAITING   111
      Mary

EPILOGUE   139

FOREWORD

I am a church-nerd, and I love Advent. I love the morning in early December when people of all ages turn up at my church and bend over long tables stacked with styrofoam rounds and pine boughs and make Advent wreaths to light at home. I love singing "Let All Mortal Flesh Keep Silent" and "O Come, O Come Emmanuel," adding another verse each week as we wind our way toward Christmas. I love praying the collect for the fourth Sunday of Advent, beseeching God to "purify our consciences by thy daily visitation, that when thy Son our Lord cometh, he may find in us a mansion prepared for himself." I want to be a mansion.

I love Advent because I am obsessed with the ecclesial calendar, with the church's seasons and the rhythm they make. I believe in church time. I think I will finally allow that I actually am a Christian, and not just aspiring to be one, when the rhythms of the church year come to me without thinking, when they come more naturally to me than the rhythms of the academic calendar (which tells me that September, not Advent, is the beginning of the year) or the rhythms of the calendar of the U.S. government (which has imprinted on my soul the four days on which self-employed people pay estimated taxes).

American culture gives us lots of cues about how to live inside time. Chiefly, we are told to spend it (have you ever noticed that almost all the verbs we pair with time are borrowed from the worlds of finance—spend, save, manage . . .). We are told, by advertisements and by our Blackberries, to squeeze time dry, to use it well, to maximize it.

The church tells us a different story about time—it is God's, and there is enough of it, more than enough. The church's narrative about time is never clearer than during Advent, when we are invited to spend our time very foolishly indeed. We are invited to wait. Just to wait.

In this winsome yet provocative Advent devotional, Paula Gooder takes us into the fraught complications of Advent waiting—waiting for Christmas, in a world that starts celebrating it months ahead of time; waiting for Jesus' birth, an event that has already happened; and waiting for the return of Christ, the consummation of God's plan (a drama that some days, we may doubt will ever happen at all, and other days, we may want to forestall as long as possible). I have worked my way through Gooder's Advent reflections, and I will look forward to rereading them each Advent for many years to come.

It is commonplace to bemoan how hard it is to wait: Americans aren't good at it—we can't stand even waiting in line, we carry credit-card debt because we can't wait to buy stuff, and so on. But actually, I think we get a lot of practice at waiting. And I don't just mean the mundane waiting I did this week—waiting for three phone calls, waiting for my nails (newly periwinkle) to dry. I mean, we wait for God. We wait better or less well, with more intention or more distraction, but we wait for God a lot. We wait for God finally to hear those prayers we say all the time for someone's cancer, for someone's heartbreak, for peace and justice in this country, this neighborhood, this family; we wait because it all seems in rather short supply, this peace and succor and health. We wait and wait and wait. Most of the year, while we wait, we also work—we work for the Kingdom of God, helping to bring it about. During Advent, we set aside some of our work and focus on the waiting. During Advent, we remember how sacred a calling is this waiting.

While sitting inside Gooder's reflections, I began to sense something I had not understood before, in any of my other Advent observances: it is not just we who wait. God is waiting, too. "The Lord wait[s], that He may be gracious unto you," says Isaiah, one of the prophets who interests Gooder most. God waits on us, for our attention, for our visits home; God waits for our vision and our ear.

"God's waiting and man's," wrote the nineteenth-century British minister Alexander MacLaren, in a reflection on Isaiah 30:18. How "bold and beautiful, that He and we should be represented as sharing the same attitude." Here, then, is something of the mystery of incarnation: God's being like us is not limited to God's taking on feet and hands and hair. God is like us in this posture of pause and expectance and anticipation and longing and wondering where we are. And so Advent is not only about our waiting for God, waiting for God to get born, waiting for God to come back. It is also a time when we enter God's waiting, God's divine waiting. And perhaps that is where the meaning of waiting gleams the most brightly of all.

HOW TO USE THIS BOOK

This book aims to offer food for thought around the theme of waiting during Advent. It is not a detailed exegesis of the text—commentaries provide much better exegesis than I could here—nor is it a practical guide to waiting. Instead, it is a series of reflections inspired by the Bible that, I hope, will stimulate you to think a little more about waiting: why we do it; what it feels like to be someone who waits; what happens when we don't wait; and why God might want us to get better at it. This book also asks questions about what it might have been like for the biblical characters to wait. It does not seek to provide answers but to open up questions and to offer new ideas and ways of looking at things.

The biblical reflections occasionally delve into the history behind the text, but, as a rule, they treat the text as it is in its final form. This is not the place to engage in detailed exploration of whether the biblical characters did or did not say what they are supposed to have said, or whether the biblical authors have changed the sources available to them. We have the text that we do and my reflections take it at face value. You will need to turn to more detailed commentaries and other scholarly works for questions of authenticity and authorship.

This book is a volume of reflections, not a "how to" manual. If you want an easy fix for a busy, impatient life, this is not the book for you, but if you want to spend Advent reflecting on waiting, thinking about what happens when you wait, and accompanying Abraham and Sarah, the prophets, John the Baptist, and Mary in their waiting, then you might find something here to interest you. When I began writing the book, I tried to include questions that would help readers, who wanted them, to apply the reflections to their own life. It soon became clear that this wouldn't work. Waiting is not something that you can learn in five, ten, or even twenty-four steps. It is a frame of mind, not an "activity," a way of being, not a list of tasks. This book aims to persuade you of the virtue of waiting but also to give you food for thought that might contribute to your life of reflection and prayer so that, in the presence of God, you might grow more fully into a way of being that is governed more by waiting than by urgency and lived more in the present than in the future. This is not a manifesto for doing nothing—waiting can be immensely active—but for changing the focus of our lives from ourselves to God and from the future to the present. Such a transformation takes time and for most of us will be our life's work, born out of years of companionship with the God who waits with us.

You will notice that, after an introductory reflection on waiting, there are four chapters: one for each week of Advent. Each chapter is divided into six sections with a brief introduction and conclusion. This allows you to read one section a day from the first day of December to Christmas Eve, or to begin four full weeks before Christmas and to read one a day (with a day off each week). The chapters can also be read all the way through if that suits your pattern better. Each chapter is focused around the biblical character most associated with each of the four candles on the Advent wreath:

- The first chapter looks at Abraham and Sarah as examples of the fathers and mothers of the faith and of people whose calling draws them into a lifetime of waiting for the fulfilment of God's promise to them;

- The second chapter explores the prophets and their expectation of God's intervention in the world that was sometimes longed for and sometimes feared;

- The third chapter turns to John the Baptist, whose ministry existed between the old and the new and pointed to things beyond himself;

- And the fourth chapter looks at Mary, whose whole life was shaped by waiting for events beyond her control.

Each of the six sections in each chapter opens with a verse that will shape the core of my reflection that follows it. This is followed with a reference to the wider Bible passage for those who would like to read the whole passage by way of preparation for that section. Each section is a reflection inspired by the biblical passage and explores the themes that occurred to me while I was studying it.

A reflection on waiting

Much to my surprise as I was writing it, the Introduction turned into an extended reflection on waiting and the biblical view of time. I had not intended to begin the book in this way, but these were the words that wanted to be written and, once they were written, it seemed important to include them, because they explain some of the concepts that underpin the biblical stories we will be exploring in the rest of the book.

I hope that some people will find the introduction valuable in exploring some of those knotty issues (like how we can wait for something that has already happened and what it means to be waiting for the end times) that hover in the background, often unexpressed, during Advent. Others, however, may find it off-putting, and to you I would like to say, ignore it! The introduction lays some foundations, but you can read the book without them. If you would rather get into the exploration of the biblical stories straightaway, then do that and skip the introduction entirely. You can, of course, read it later—or indeed not at all—if that is more helpful.

THE MEANING IS
IN THE WAITING

A REFLECTION ON WAITING

KNEELING

Moments of great calm,
Kneeling before an altar
Of wood in a stone church
In summer, waiting for the God
To speak; the air a staircase
For silence; the sun's light
Ringing me, as though I acted
A great role. And the audiences
Still; all that close throng
Of spirits waiting, as I,
For the message.
Prompt me, God;
But not yet. When I speak,
Though it be you who speak
Through me, something is lost.
The meaning is in the waiting.

R.S. THOMAS

Why wait?

Imagine entering a room and finding a beautifully wrapped present on a table. Attached to the present is a label that reads: "This present is for you but don't open it now . . . wait."

An instruction like this might evoke a wide range of emotions, but probably the two most common would be a sense of indignation or frustration and/or a tingle of anticipation. Depending on who we are, we might feel just one emotion—entirely irritated or completely intrigued—but I, at least, would have a complex combination of the two: irritation tinged with anticipation or eagerness laced with frustration.

In reality, I wonder how many of us would obey the command to wait. Waiting is not something most of us do easily. Our frustrations at waiting begin at an early age and are hard to outgrow. When I tell my own children to wait, and see on their faces that familiar expression that borders on emotional agony, I recognize it, not so much because I remember feeling that way when I was their age—although I do—but because I still feel that way now and am less able to express it quite so openly.

Antipathy to waiting is exacerbated, if not encouraged, by the world in which we live. All around us we encounter, day after day, the encouragement not to wait but to have what we want now. Our credit-driven society urges us to abandon all thought of waiting and to buy now; so many advertisements have as their underlying message "why wait?" Improvements in communication only erode the notion of waiting further. We are told that people feel aggrieved if they have to wait for more than twenty-four hours to receive a reply from an e-mail, and mobile phones help us to be available even when we are away from home. Waiting is increasingly a strange notion. We have become accustomed to immediacy and swift action.

Given all of this, it seems almost ludicrous that the church should have Advent, four weeks dedicated to waiting. Is this not the church, yet again, looking backward to bygone days, to ideas irrelevant to our society, out of touch and out of date? Would it not be a better idea to abandon Advent altogether? There are some who would argue that in effect we have already done so. Barely a year goes by without people telling stories of the time when Advent really was Advent: when Christmas trees were set up on Christmas Eve and not before; when Christmas carols were, likewise, sung on Christmas Eve and for the following days of Christmas—and not in November. When this happened, we are told, Advent could be properly Advent and Christmas, Christmas; and we weren't all fed up with Christmas by the twenty-fifth of December.

What seems to have happened is that the tingle of anticipation, that looking forward to Christmas brings, has encouraged us to "anticipate" Christmas in another sense, not in the sense of "look forward to" but in the sense of "bringing it forward and beginning celebrations early." This is certainly true in shops where, as people often observe, Christmas decorations seem to appear earlier and earlier every year so that we have barely returned from our summer holidays when we are entangled in yards of tinsel. Preparation for Christmas means, for many people, beginning Christmas early. I was amazed last year to find a box of mince pies in a supermarket in September, with a consume-by date of the end of October. Not only were we to buy our mince pies early, we were to eat them early too.

On celebrating Advent

So what are we to do? It might appear that the only solution is for churches to become guardians of Christmas and of Advent: to issue edicts banning the singing of Christmas carols and the eating of mince pies before the twenty-fourth of December; to patrol people's houses to insure that they do not set up their Christmas trees too early, insuring that Christmas does not begin before its time. This would hardly be popular or desirable. Culture and expectations have changed, and the celebration of Christmas is now widely accepted as beginning at least halfway through December if not even earlier. It appears curmudgeonly to insist on beginning Christmas at the "right" time and it is almost certainly a fruitless exercise.

Does this mean, therefore, that we should abandon Advent? Should we simply accept that Advent is no longer in tune with our culture and abandon all pretence of observing it, with the possible exception of the odd chocolate-laden Advent calendar? Obviously not, but it does raise the question of *how* we celebrate Advent in a way that enhances the season and the month of December and that enables us to "anticipate" Christmas properly in the sense of looking forward to it, preparing ourselves, and becoming ready, rather than in the sense of starting early.

An active waiting in the present

Part of the clue to a reinvigorated and renewed vision of Advent lies in waiting; a waiting that rests not in frustration but in stillness; not in frenzied anticipation but in an embracing of the present. If we want to appreciate Advent fully, we need to relearn how to wait, to rediscover the art of savoring the future, of staying in the present and of finding meaning in the act of waiting.

It was only when I was pregnant with my first child that I realized that I had completely misunderstood what waiting was about. I have a very low boredom threshold and, consequently, am very bad at waiting. Waiting makes me anxious, restless, and uneasy. Imagine my bemusement then to encounter an experience that is entirely about waiting. No one who is expecting a child wants the waiting to end and the baby to come early—that can only spell heartache. The only thing to do in pregnancy is to wait, and not only that but to hope against hope that the period of waiting does not end prematurely. It was during this period of enforced waiting that I began to discover that waiting is not just about passing the time between the moment when expectation is raised and when it comes to completion—in this instance between conception and birth—but that it has deep and lasting value in and of itself.

As I waited for the birth of my baby, I discovered that waiting can be a nurturing time, valuable in its own right. Until then, I had assumed that waiting could only be passive, that it involved sitting around, drumming my fingers, completely powerless to do anything until the moment of waiting passed and I could be active again. How wrong I was. The waiting of pregnancy is about as active an occupation as one can hope to engage in. Pregnant waiting is a profoundly creative act, involving a slow growth to new life. This kind of waiting may appear passive externally but internally consists of never-ending action and is a helpful analogy for the kind of waiting that Advent requires. For many of us, Advent is such a busy time with all our preparations for Christmas that the thought of stopping and sitting passively—while attractive in many ways—is simply impossible. Advent, however, does not demand passivity but the utmost activity: active internal waiting that knits together new life.

One of the other things I learned during pregnancy was that learning to savor the time of waiting allows us also to appreciate the event when it comes. The loss of an ability to wait often brings with it the inability to be fully and joyfully present now. Instead, we are constantly looking backward to better times we used to know and forward to better times that may be coming. The more we do this, the more we miss the present. Not only that, but it becomes hard to appreciate the future moment even when it does come. Many people speak of the feeling of deep anticlimax on Christmas Day when that long-anticipated day does not live up to expectations. Often the reason for this is that we live forever in the future, so that, when the future becomes the present, we are ill-equipped to deal with it and have lost the ability to be fully present, right now.

One of the many reasons we wait in Advent is to hone our skills of being joyfully and fully present now. After a month of doing this, Christmas Day can gain a depth and meaning that would otherwise fly past in a whirl of presents and mince pies.

Such deep attention to the present cannot help but transform us as we learn—or relearn as the case may be—how to live deeply and truly in the present moment, so that we are content to linger in our lives as they are now and not be forever looking forward, striving onward to the next goal. This introduction began with R.S. Thomas's famous poem "Kneeling," from which the title of this book is drawn. In it he articulates the fact that sometimes the really profound moments of our lives occur "in between" at that moment just before something happens: truth lurks in the moment between the out breath and the in breath or in the moment just before someone speaks. As Thomas recognizes in his poem, the paradox is that sometimes the fulfillment of that for which we wait robs us of what we were waiting for and that we discover to our surprise that the meaning is in the waiting and not in the fulfillment.

Once we recognize this, it becomes clear that Advent is not an irrelevant, cultural dinosaur but is vital for our very well-being. If we are able, during Advent, to relearn the skill of waiting, then it will have value not only for Advent and Christmas, but for the whole of our lives. Advent offers us a gift of such importance that it is life transforming; it is not so much a season as a way of being. As is often the case with the festivals of the church's year, in Advent we are invited into a deeper, truer encounter with ourselves, with the world, and, most of all, with God. Although learning the lessons of the season will help us to celebrate the season better, even more important is the fact that they polish our skills, sharpen our insight, and deepen our walk with God in such a way that the whole of our life is affected. Advent invites us to focus on, learn, and relearn a skill essential to our Christian journey.

Waiting for the past

Recognizing the importance of waiting, however, does not solve all our problems with Advent waiting. One of the oddest features of Advent is that it requires us to wait for something that has already happened, as well as for something that has not. It is the double vision of Advent that we look both backward with expectation as we wait for the birth of Christ 2,000 years ago and also forward with anticipation to the end times. The awkwardness of Advent is enhanced by the expectation that we not only wait for the past, which seems impossible, but also for the end times—a doctrine that many people find increasingly uncomfortable and hard to talk about.

The clue to understanding the requirements of Advent-waiting lies in the Bible and the biblical view of history. One of the features that often confuses people when they read the Bible is the fact that it appears to conflate different events into a single time. Take for example Psalm 74:12–17:

> Yet God my King is from of old,
>> working salvation in the earth.
> You divided the sea by your might;
>> you broke the heads of the dragons
>> in the waters.
> You crushed the heads of Leviathan;
>> you gave him as food for the
>> creatures of the wilderness.
> You cut openings for springs and torrents;
>> you dried up ever-flowing streams.
> Yours is the day, yours also the night;
>> you established the luminaries and the sun.
> You have fixed all the bounds of the earth;
>> you made summer and winter.

What event is being referred to in this passage? The passage is resonant of creation. The reference to God's breaking the heads of the dragons and crushing the head of Leviathan may refer to an ancient and alternative version of the creation account in which God wrestled dragons during the act of creation. Alongside this rather odd reference we also have the much more familiar reference to God's establishing the luminaries and the sun, fixing the bounds of the earth, and making summer and winter. On one level, these verses refer to God as creator. If we go back and look again, however, the reference to dividing the sea with your might and drying up ever-flowing streams seems to be a reference to the crossing of the Red Sea. Yet one more reading of the passage seems to suggest an allusion to Moses striking the rock in the wilderness to produce a stream of water in "you cut openings for springs and torrents." So which is it? Which of these biblical events lies behind this passage? The answer is all of them.

Verse 12 describes God as "working salvation in the earth." This conflated account of God's working of salvation indicates that in the mind of the psalmist these are all effectively the same event, or at least so close as to be regarded as overlapping. This is bemusing to us because our view of history is almost completely different from this. Modern, western twenty-first-century views of history largely regard history as linear. What this means is that at one end of the line is creation, at the other is the end of the world, and we are placed upon this line somewhere between the beginning and the end. History proceeds along the line in a single direction, and we can never go back. The biblical view of history appears to differ from this. Salvation history is not so much linear as cyclical. The telling of the history of God's interaction with the world is probably best likened to a snowball, if that image is not too odd. Imagine making a snowball at the top of a hill and then pushing it to make it roll down the hill to the bottom. As the snowball descends it rolls round and round, picking up more snow as it goes. The snowball is still the same, though it gets larger as it rolls. Salvation history is a little like this. God's interventions in the world are regarded as similar events, if not the same one. Each time this occurs, God's act of salvation picks up another resonance or expression so that the psalmist can in all honesty describe God's salvation in terms of the odd mix of creation, the crossing of the Red Sea, and the wilderness tradition.

This also makes much more sense of the descriptions of Jesus in the Gospels. People are often bemused and a little troubled that Jesus is portrayed in the Gospels in terms of events from the Hebrew Scriptures of the Old Testament. The suggestion made by some is that this means the stories about Jesus have been fabricated. Much more likely is the fact that the Gospel writers are standing in this same tradition of biblical salvation history that sees Jesus' presence on earth as yet one more—though even more wonderful—example of God's intervention in the world. Thus Jesus' presence *is* creation, Exodus, return from exile (and much more), all rolled into one glorious snowball of salvation.

This is relevant in Advent, because it consequently becomes possible to wait for the past. The snowball of history rolls ever onward: the layer of snow that is Jesus' ministry is particularly rich and deep, but is not the end. Salvation history continues today. The point of telling and retelling the history of salvation is so that we can recognize it when it breaks into our world. The message of salvation history is that God *is* the kind of God who breaks into our world: creating, liberating, healing, raising from the dead, and saving. God has done it so often through history, and because the snowball rolls on, will do so again, but we need to train ourselves to be able to recognize that creation/Exodus/return from exile/birth of Jesus/resurrection moment when it appears before our eyes. So often God is present in our world, but we fail to recognize it. Elizabeth Barrett Browning summed this up in her poem "Aurora Leigh":

> Earth's crammed with heaven,
> And every common bush afire with God;
> But only he who sees, takes off his shoes—
> The rest sit round it and pluck blackberries.

It seems a natural part of human nature that we are more predisposed to sit around and pluck blackberries (or the modern equivalent) than to perceive the presence of God, take off our shoes, and worship.

This can be as true for those of us who want to perceive God's presence as for those who do not. It can be that, despite our best intentions, shimmers of divine presence are overlooked or misinterpreted; we see something that proclaims God's presence in our midst but fail to recognize it for what it is. Part of the purpose of the telling, retelling, and telling again of the history of salvation throughout the Old Testament and into the New is to train us to recognize what it looks like, so that when it does happen again, we not only notice it but understand what it is. The Hebrew word that is often translated *wait* (as in Genesis 49:18, "I wait for your salvation, O LORD") has the additional meaning of "look eagerly" or "lie in wait for" that brings with it that concept of being a "lookout" whose sole task is to gaze into the distance, waiting for a particular person to come, and then, when they do come, to be able to distinguish them from the others who come the same way. The telling and retelling of God's saving acts is one way in which we can begin to recognize that longed-for figure, even when they are still a speck on the horizon.

In Advent, then, we wait for something that has already happened in sure and certain knowledge that it will happen again, and again, and again. It is this certainty that underpins the New Testament concept of hope. In current speech, hope is a vague optimistic feeling: "I hope I'll see you tomorrow." For the biblical writers, hope carries with it a sense of certainty. As the writer to the Hebrews puts it: "We have this hope, a sure and steadfast anchor of the soul" (6:19). This is no fuzzy, good wish but a clear, concrete assertion of reality based, as is so much of Hebrews, in a careful rehearsal of the past, as a means of living well in the present and for the future.

Waiting for the future

The final dimension of Advent that remains, as yet, unexplored is our waiting for the future. The great Advent hymns like "Lo, he comes with clouds descending" point forward to a time in the future when Jesus will return to judge the earth. Indeed, what is believed to be the original version of the hymn as first written by John Cennick (1718–55) has a verse that reads:

> Every island, sea, and mountain,
> Heav'n and Earth shall flee away;
> All who hate Him must, confounded
> Hear the trump proclaim the day:
> Come to Judgment! Come to judgment!
>   Come to judgment! Come away!

A similar verse can be found in Charles Wesley's even more popular edited version, published in 1758. Although the whole hymn focuses on the end times, this verse brings out the theme of judgment much more clearly than the rest of the hymn; it is, perhaps, telling that neither Cennick's original nor Wesley's edited verse are commonly included when we sing this hymn during Advent.

For many people the theme of end times and judgment is the equivalent of an embarrassing relative—still present but best ignored. There are two problems that we encounter with beliefs about the end of the world: one is that, despite the active expectation of the earliest Christians, it still hasn't happened; and the other is the gory emphasis on judgment that many find distasteful (an emphasis that is only exacerbated by medieval paintings of the Day of Judgment with all their blood and scenes of agony).

So what are we to do? The most common response to the problems of end-times theology appears to be a quiet ignoring of the theme. With magnificent elegance we ignore the enormous elephant in the room, even when Advent magnifies it so large that our faces are pressed into its sides. Of course, not everyone does ignore the end times, and the interpretation of the end of the world that can be found in certain types of theology—often originating in the United States, and expressed in popular writing such as the Left Behind series—does nothing to encourage those who would rather not talk about it to address the issue.

There is no easy answer to the problem, but ignoring it is, in my view, possibly the worst of all solutions. Removing all traces of end-times theology from our preaching and discussion makes a nonsense not only of our Advent hymns, that proclaim it with such fervour, but of the Bible itself. It is simply not possible to make sense of the biblical themes of justification, salvation, resurrection, kingdom of God, and so on without an accompanying theology of the end; or, to be more accurate, to remove a theology of the end from these themes alters them so radically that they are no longer the themes raised and discussed by Jesus and the earliest Christian communities.

The reappropriation of end-times theology in a way that makes sense of it today is such a large theme that it would require a whole book (if not a series of them) to discuss it properly. Consequently, I intend here to raise one issue that might help us address this vexed Advent question. One of the things that Advent does is invite us to inhabit the biblical worldview of time and of the end. Just as waiting for the past invites us to abandon our sequential model of history in favor of one shaped more like a rolling snowball, so waiting for the future invites us to inhabit a world shaped and informed by a vision of the end. When we do so, we discover some profound answers to our questions, alongside the numerous problems.

The answers proffered by a biblical view of the end speak into the heart of a troubled world shot through with glimmers of God's glory. Why is it that despite our best efforts and determined repentance we cannot act as we wish we could? Why is it that Christian communities experience as much conflict as others do? Why is it that despite the evident presence of God in our midst we get ground down by the events of the world we live in? For the biblical writers, and particularly Paul, the key to understanding this lies in Jesus' resurrection and its connection to the end times. There were many views of resurrection in the period of Jesus—including the Sadducean view that it would not happen—but where people did believe in it, they were generally agreed that it would take place at the end times on the Day of Judgment.

The significance of Jesus' resurrection (as opposed to the miracles in the Gospels involving the raising of people like Lazarus, who, unlike Jesus, would die again at some point) was that he alone has been raised beforehand. For writers like Luke and Paul this meant that the end times had already begun but had not yet come to completion. God's kingdom had broken in but only partially; the experience of reconciliation in the new creation was now possible, but creation still groaned with longing for its completion. In other words, we are between: between the beginning of the end and the end of the end. This explains why we can have a vision of the world as God yearns for it to be but not the ability to bring it about in full. We can catch a glimpse of human relationship shaped by generous, mutual support but have to live with the reality that this happens only occasionally. In other words, we see glimmers of God's glory in the world but have to wait for the time when that glory will suffuse the whole of creation.

This biblical vision of waiting for the future is one that calls forth both an acceptance of the reality of our current situation and a determination to change it. We live "between" and so must accept the nature of the world as it is now, but we can also grasp hold of God's possibility for the world. The glimmers of God's glory that we see exist to strengthen our resolve to increase those glimmers, to strive to make God's kingdom more present on earth every day. Waiting for the future involves a recognition of what the world might be and the resolve to bring our own part of it one step closer. Yet again waiting becomes active: waiting for the future involves transforming the present.

As I have already said, this does not make many people's problems with beliefs about the end of the world any easier, but it does remind us what we stand to lose if we abandon the concept entirely. Without a belief in the end times, we lose a theological explanation of the almost-but-not-quite sense that fills so much of Christian experience. We know what could happen, even what ought to happen but cannot quite get there. Belief in the end times is both forgiving (it can't happen in its fullness because we aren't there yet) and inspiring (we are aiming for a time when the world will be transformed—so keep on trying—it is worth it).

The element of future waiting in Advent collapses time just as waiting for the past does. Entering the biblical worldview, which focuses on the future culmination in glory of all our present suffering and woe, changes the present because it invites us to strive to make real in the present a little of that glorious future held open for us through the past death and resurrection of Jesus. The concept is mind-blowing, and we will almost certainly fail to grasp it in all its fullness in this life, but grappling with it is, in my view, part of what Advent invites us to do.

On waiting

Advent, then, calls us into a state of active waiting: a state that recognizes and embraces the glimmers of God's presence in the world, that recalls and celebrates God's historic yet ever present actions, that speaks the truth about the almost-but-not-quite nature of our Christian living, that yearns for but cannot quite achieve divine perfection. Most of all, Advent summons us to the present moment, to a still yet active, a tranquil yet steadfast commitment to the life we live now. It is this to which Advent beckons us, and without it our Christian journey is impoverished.

■

ONE

CALLED TO WAIT

Abraham and Sarah,
Our Ancestors in the Faith

INTRODUCTION

Traditionally, each of the candles on an Advent wreath is associated with a character or characters in the long run-up to Jesus' life, who show us something of what the wait for Jesus entails. The first Advent candle is associated with the "patriarchs," a word that comes from the Greek for father, *pater*, and for leader, *archon*. Originally, therefore, a patriarch was the leader of a tribe—the father of an extended family grouping who acted as their leader. Within the Hebrew Scriptures of the Old Testament the term is normally used to describe Abraham, Isaac, and Jacob, because their story is essentially a family history, in which the family is gathered around a single father figure or patriarch. The association of this candle with Abraham has added to the patriarchs the element of faith (because Abraham's story is essentially a story of faith, a theme that Paul picked up so clearly in Romans 4), so that they are called "the patriarchs of the faith," with the emphasis that they are, in some way, our own fathers in the faith.

One of the most surprising elements of the stories about Abraham, Isaac, and Jacob is the significant role played by their wives: Sarah, Rebekah, and Rachel respectively. In a culture where women had little, if any, influence, these women shape the stories of the patriarchs by their presence in them. Like their husbands, Sarah, Rebekah, and Rachel sometimes behave well and sometimes badly, but their role in the unfolding story of the family of God is vital. An exploration of the patriarchs, therefore, also brings with it an exploration of the matriarchs, whose lives are entwined, in faith, with our own.

Some people take the patriarchs' candle to include the whole sweep of Israelite history from Abraham to David, when the prophets can then take over and continue until John the Baptist. Tempting as it is to adopt this view, since it would open up a treasure trove of the best stories from the Hebrew Scriptures, I shall restrict myself to Abraham, whose ancestry in the faith points us to a quality of waiting that seems particularly relevant to Advent.

We begin with Abram's call to leave with Sarai and the rest of his close family and follow God (their names change to the more familiar Abraham and Sarah only later in the story).

> *"Go from your country and your kindred and your father's house to the land that I will show you."*

GENESIS 12:1

FOR FURTHER READING
Genesis 12:1–9

Imagine the conversation:

"Er, Sarai, dear."
"Yes, Abram."
"I've just had a word from God."
"How nice for you."
"God's told us to leave everything and go."
"Oh . . . so where are we going?"
"Ah well, . . . I don't know yet, but God will
    tell us when we get there."

So what does Sarai say next? Of course, this conversation is entire projection. In Abram's culture, no such conversation would or could take place. Sarai would just be told that they were going, but it does raise the important question of what the people of the Bible might say back to God at moments that we think are inspirational.

We are so familiar with this story that it is easy to miss the impact of God's command to Abram, that boils down to "leave everything that you know and love, and go somewhere. I'm not going to tell you where yet, but when you get there I'll let you know."

Of course, this command does not have the same level of impact on Abram as it might on us. It seems as though Abram's family might already have been semi-nomadic (that is, they moved from one settled life to another settled life, as opposed to fully nomadic, which involves constant moving) since in Genesis 11:31 (two verses before this one), we are told that Terah, Abram's father, had already moved the family from Ur to Haran (a distance of about 600 miles). Nevertheless, the extent of what God was asking of Abram is made clear in the command that he issued to Abram to leave behind:

- *Your land*: this is often translated as *country* which seems to imply something about nationality. In fact the word is much bigger, and smaller, than this. The Hebrew word, *aretz*, refers to dry land, as opposed to water like the sea or rivers, and in creation God separated the waters from the dry land (*aretz*) to make a place for plants, animals, and humans to dwell (Genesis 1:11). It also refers to the bit of land upon which you dwell and so is connected to your livelihood but also to your roots. Land symbolized not only sustenance but belonging.

- *Your relatives*: literally this is connected to the verb *to be born* and therefore involves all those born around you and hence refers to your relatives. This then is a command to leave the everyday networks of relationships that governed Abram's life.

- *Your father's house*: here we see that we have moved from the larger to the smaller unit: from land, that governs a general sustenance and sense of belonging, to relatives, who provided a network of relationship and identity, to your father's house, which is where Abram lived.

Abram is commanded to leave them all from the greatest to the smallest. All of Abram's ties are to be cut, from the universal to the specific, from the abstract to the concrete, from general living to day-to-day existence. Abram is to leave them all and "go."

The word *go* brings challenges of its own. Abram is to journey away from all that he knows, to leave it all behind and go . . . somewhere. It appears to stand in great contrast to Jesus' call to discipleship "come, follow me" (Matthew 19:21). Abram's call is to leave; Jesus' call is to arrive, though, in reality, that contrast is not there in the Hebrew. The word used in God's command to Abram is the word that can also be used for come. It depends on where you are standing. If you are with the person then the command is to go, but if you stand a way off and call, then the command is to come.

With God the command is both to go and to come. The "go" element involves leaving behind many things; the command to "come" involves knowing that God will accompany us on the journey. Within Christian circles, the technical word *vocation* has come to mean a specific call (at a certain time in someone's life) to a very specific task (often ordination, though it is used of other callings as well). This can obscure the fact that God is always calling us and that part of the nature of God's call is this double calling to go and to come; to leave behind and to accompany God on the way. With Abram, God's call was certainly to a lifetime of accompanying God. In verse 1, God tells Abram to go to the land that God would show him; in verse 7 God shows him the land ("To your offspring I will give this land"), but then Abram traveled on to Bethel, to the Negeb, down to Egypt, and back again. God's initial call, then, wasn't just to a single act of traveling with an early, fixed end point but to a frame of mind, one that is prepared to "leave behind" and to "accompany."

Abram's call is really a call to waiting. As we will see when the story unfolds, Abram is promised great things, but he doesn't really see the fruits of this promise in his lifetime. There are seeds: he is shown the land that will belong to his descendants, and after much heartache he does have a son through whom the line will be preserved, but these seeds remain just that, seeds, until his death. So I return to my desire to hear what Abram thought of all this. At the end of his life did he look back and decide that the lifetime of wandering, of leaving, of accompanying, and of waiting was worthwhile or not?

We will never know, but what we can know is how we respond in such circumstances. God's call to us remains a call to change: to leaving and accompanying, to moving and changing, to growing and flourishing. It is part of human nature to yearn for stability, to put down roots, and to stay put; but it is also a rule of nature that things that do not move do not live. Water that does not move becomes stagnant, and in the same way when we do not move we become sluggish and hard to change. God's call does not necessarily ask us to move our physical surroundings (although sometimes it does); most often it asks us to move our internal surroundings, to be prepared to be changed and transformed.

The voice that spoke to Abram still speaks to us: "Go, from the things that bind you, from the sense of your own identity, from your day-to-day way of being to something that I shall show you."

God calls, and waits for our response. . . .

"Do not be afraid, Abram, I am your shield;
your reward shall be very great."
But Abram said, "O Lord GOD,
what will you give me, for I continue childless,
and the heir of my house is Eliezer of Damascus?"

GENESIS 15:1–2

FOR FURTHER READING
Genesis 15:1–21

We may never hear what Abram really thought
about being told to leave everything, but in this passage I
do get my wish of finding out what he thinks once he has
left. In verse 2 Abram responds, when God speaks to him
again at the start of Genesis 15, and it is hard to work out
whether to be encouraged or depressed by it. In chapter
12 Abram appeared to respond so well, he was prepared
to leave everything behind and to go with God, without
any clear idea about where he was going other than that
God would show him the way. Here, however, we find
a much more human response—the kind I would give—
and that is why I can't decide whether to be pleased or
depressed that he was, in fact, as impatient as I am. The
issue is that Abram seems to miss the point that God is
making here.

God says three things to Abram:

- "Don't be afraid."
- "I am your shield."
- "Your reward will be very great."

Don't be afraid

The command not to be afraid comes with astonishing regularity in the Bible. Nearly every appearance of angels and many visions of God are accompanied with the encouragement not to fear. This encouragement is necessary, because fear is the appropriate response in the presence of God. The Hebrew Scriptures have a strand running through them that speaks of God as so holy, so awesome, and so other that fear is the only emotion possible in God's presence. Often, within the Christian tradition, fear has been replaced by intimacy; the strand of God's great love for the world has overlaid the tradition of fear. The paradox of God's relationship with us, however, is that it contains love *and* danger, intimacy *and* fear. God loves us with an all-embracing, deep, and passionate love: a love that is as warming as fire—and as dangerous. It is appropriate then that Abram should be afraid, and God's word comes with reassurance of his safety in the powerful, fearful presence of God.

Abram's response, however, suggests that his fear is not actually about this. His immediate anxiety seems to be more about whether God's promise will in fact be fulfilled. His answer to God's word to him seems to imply that his fear is as much about getting what he has been promised as it is about the fact that he is in conversation with a holy and powerful God. Despite his bold following of God and his apparent fearless abandonment of all his ties in chapter 12, Abram now seems anxious. In response to God's words of encouragement in verse 1, in the next verse Abram points out all the difficulties: God hasn't given him anything yet, he has no children, and someone else will inherit from him unless he does.

This pattern of boldness followed by doubts is a common one in the Bible. Perhaps the best example of it is in the story of the Exodus (Exodus chapters 12–16), where the people of God follow Moses boldly through the Red Sea and out of Egypt. Almost immediately on the other side, they start to grumble: it was better in Egypt, there was food there, and they knew where they were. In a similar way here, Abram has done what was asked of him, but he hasn't yet got what he wanted, and so he is afraid.

I am your shield

God's word to Abram anticipates all of Abram's anxieties. Not only is Abram told not to fear, a reason is given for this lack of fear: God is his shield. Although not the most common image of God in the Hebrew Scriptures, the depiction of God as a shield does occur on numerous occasions. In Deuteronomy 33:29 God is described as "the shield of your help," and in 2 Samuel 22:31 as "a shield for all who take refuge in him." Alongside the image of God as dangerous presence runs the image of God as protector; the one who will shield his people from harm. This image does not promise that no harm will happen; shields do not prevent wars, but they do protect a soldier from arrows.

Your reward will be very great

Abram's other reason not to fear is because he will receive his reward, and when he does so, it will be enormous. Abram's response reveals that, perhaps, he too struggles with waiting. His response in verse 2 runs along the lines of "that's all very well but I can't see what you can do because I have no children," with an accompanying implication that in any case God has already promised him a lot, and he hasn't seen any changes yet. Abram's view may not, in reality, be that different from ours: he thought that it was impossible for God to do anything to change the situation and assumed that because nothing *had* changed, nothing could change.

What is interesting is that Abram only responds to the last thing that God says: "your reward will be very great." The two earlier and much more important phrases "don't be afraid" and "I am your shield" appear to pass him by as he focuses on the reward, what it will be and, when he will get it. He skipped over God's promise of company, support, and refuge in the present and focused on what might be coming to him in the future. Abram finds himself caught here between what was and what will be, and seems unable to rest in confidence with the God who is.

God continues to speak to us in the same way: "Do not be afraid, I am your refuge," and yearns that we might stay a while with the "God who is," rather than rushing after a future reward, however great it may be.

Sarai said to Abram, "You see that the LORD *has prevented me from bearing children; go in to my slave-girl; it may be that I shall obtain children by her." And Abram listened to the voice of Sarai.*

GENESIS 16:2

FOR FURTHER READING
Genesis 16:1–16

Imagine you have a broken washing machine. You call the washing machine repair service and wait, and wait, and wait, but no one comes. In your desperation, you get out the tool kit and attempt to solve the problem yourself. Now *you* may be a brilliant repairer of washing machines, but I know that I would end up with a pile of parts on the floor, no washing machine, and the need to go out and buy a new one. The story of Sarai and Hagar in chapter 16 is like this, only ten times worse because the destruction affected lives and not just metal.

By chapter 16, the anxiety that we saw in Abram in Genesis 15 has evidently grown rather than diminished. Despite the somewhat spectacular covenant ceremony that took place at the end of Genesis 15 (involving cutting animals in two and a smoking fire pot passing between the two halves), that should have allayed Abram's fears about the future in the certain knowledge that God would keep his side of the bargain, Genesis 16 opens with a deeply anxious conversation between Sarai and Abram about the fact that she cannot have children.

From our vantage point thousands of years later, it is easy to judge Sarai for her lack of trust in God's promise, but the cards were stacked against her: we are told that she cannot conceive children, that they had been in the land for *ten years* and that she is old (or at least this is implied—in 16:16 Abram is said to be eighty-six, which if we count backward from the ages given in 17:17 makes Sarai seventy-five). In short, Sarai, and Abram with her, had given up hope. Anyone who has struggled to conceive a child can understand the desperation of Sarai and Abram. The waiting, the flickers of hope, followed by the despair of knowing that yet again it was not to be, are enough to turn anyone to desperate actions. The problem, of course, with desperate actions is living with their consequences.

Sarai's solution to the lack of the fulfillment of God's promise to Abram was to solve it themselves: half a promise seemed better than no promise. Her solution was to conceive a child that belonged to Abram though not to Sarai. On the surface, this seems such a good idea, and Sarai's passing comment directs our attention to what she hoped would happen: that any child born to the slave she owned would become her own child. Surrogacy, which was in fact quite common in the ancient world, was made all the more necessary because of the shame that was loaded on to women when they could not conceive. A similar situation arises for Sarai's granddaughter-in-law Rachel who likewise could not conceive and likewise suggested her slave, Bilhah, as a surrogate for her (30:3) and likewise had to live with the strife of family discord that resulted from the decision.

In fact, surrogacy was so very common that one of the ancient law codes—the Code of Hammurabi, one of the earliest law codes from Babylon—states that when a concubine acts as a surrogate and then claims equality with her mistress, she should be made a slave once more. It is possible that the depth of Sarai's anger about the situation arose because she was brought up in a land that recognized the Hammurabi code and supported mistresses over slaves, but now found herself in a foreign land, Canaan, with no such provision and with an Egyptian slave girl, Hagar, who did not recognize the rules of her childhood.

Whatever the background of her hurt and anger, Sarai, with permission from Abram, treated Hagar badly. The Hebrew word translated "harshly" here can mean either to afflict or to humble and may imply that Sarai attempted to enact the Hammurabi code herself. The ensuing misery that Hagar experienced caused her to run away and although this time she returned—sent back with promise of protection from God—she was subsequently evicted by Abram once Isaac was born and was once more saved by God in the desert (21:14–21).

The tragedy of this story is that the lives of Abram, Sarai, Hagar, and Ishmael were all blighted by the fact that Sarai attempted a shortcut to the promises of God. However much we feel for Sarai's desperation for a child and the fulfillment of God's promise, we cannot avoid the fact that her actions, condoned by Abram, would have destroyed the lives of two bystanders if God had not stepped in to save them.

This story highlights one of the problems that arise when we cannot or will not wait. Sarai's solution was a good one on the face of it: it solved the problem of Abram's lack of a child and appeared to make a step toward the fulfillment of God's promise. The problem was that Sarai could only see as far as her immediate need; she had no concept of how she would feel if her plan was successful (when Hagar looked at her with contempt) or of how her plan might impact the lives of others. Immediate action often only resolves immediate need, but can set up a chain of consequences far beyond our comprehension.

Waiting draws us into a different way of being that does not rush to easy answers—that often have complex consequences—but takes account of not just our own welfare but that of all those around us. Waiting involves seeing differently and recognizing that quick answers are not always the best ones.

"No longer shall your name be Abram, but your name shall be Abraham; for I have made you the ancestor of a multitude of nations . . ." God said to Abraham, "As for Sarai your wife, you shall not call her Sarai, but Sarah shall be her name."

GENESIS 17:5 AND 15

FOR FURTHER READING
Genesis 17:1–15

What's in a name? Well quite a lot really. For those of you who, like me, remember *Opal Fruits* and *Marathons*, they will always be Opal Fruits and Marathons and not *Starbursts* and *Snickers*. Names are really quite important, because they communicate something more than just a string of letters. The words *Opal Fruits* still communicate to me a tangy taste, a need to chew, and the disappointment that it went so fast that you had to have another; whereas the word *Starbursts* communicates to me very little at all. Realistically, who could name their children after someone they really didn't like?

As the biblical writers knew all too well, a name was very much more than just the letters from which it was made. Names and the meaning of names are important in the Bible. A person's name communicated something about them: who they were, what they were like, even what would happen to them. Changing someone's name was significant because it signaled not only a change in what you called them but what they were like and what would happen to them.

In this second account of the creating of a covenant with Abram, the promise is accompanied by action on both sides: God changed Abram's and Sarai's names, as a symbol of what would happen to them in the future, and Abram undertook to circumcise both himself and the rest of his family, as a symbol of his acceptance of the covenant. This change of name is significant, though a little confusing. Genesis 17 declares that God is changing Abram's name to Abraham, because God has made him the ancestor of many nations. Nice and straightforward until one pauses a moment to consider the Hebrew.

Abram is formed from *ab*, which means *father*, and *ram*, which means *exalted*, so it means something roughly like "father of exaltation," though whether this refers to Abram himself or to God isn't clear. The problem exists in the name Abraham, which simply seems to be an expansion of Abram. There is no evidence that *raham* meant *multitude* in biblical Hebrew. A possible explanation is that a word meaning *multitude* and looking like Abraham did exist at some point but is now lost; another is that it is a play on *hamon* that does exist and does mean *multitude*. It is not hugely important except that it draws attention to the fact that what a name means is as important within the Bible as whose name it is.

My favorite biblical name change, however, is that of Sarai to Sarah. Sarai and Sarah are, in fact, the same name in Hebrew, both mean *princess*. No *significant* change is made by God, but the subtle change is important: in Hebrew, Sarai sounds very like *tzarai* which means *my distress*. The effect of the name change is to keep the name the same but to move it from sounding like *my distress* to *princess* alone. The tenderness that surrounds such a shift is powerful and affective: Sarah, whose life has been shaped by so much distress and disappointment, is now only to be remembered as a princess. God's changing of Abram's and Sarai's names to Abraham and Sarah signals his intent. His promise is now bound into their identities; everyone who utters their new names will remember God's promise to them.

The change of name also serves as consolation. If the timings in the story are to be relied upon at all (though we have to acknowledge that the time spans are, to say the least, excessive), Abraham and Sarah have now been traveling for a very long time. Abraham is ninety-nine, he was eighty-six when Ishmael was born, and we are told that they had been in Canaan at that point for ten years. That means that they have been waiting, following God, but also getting more and more anxious for twenty-six years. Even a moment's thought tells us of the strain, the distress, and anxiety that this must have caused them. It is into this situation that God's change of their names comes—a symbol of something more; a promise of the future. When parents name their children, it is an act of hope for all that their lives might be, but when an adult's name is changed, it is something much more certain—a recognition of identity and a promise of the future.

It seems somewhat odd that God does not, at this point, put them out of their misery and give them a son, rather than another, if more intimate, promise. No explanation is given for this, just the merest hint that more waiting is needed, that God's promise cannot quite come to fruition because . . . ? Who knows what the reason was? It is easy to rush to blame Abraham or Sarah for their treatment of Hagar, but the real reason remains a mystery. It is just possible, however, that the waiting is what is important. It was not intended as divine torture but as gift; though, embroiled as they were in the future promise, it was a gift that Abraham and Sarah could not grasp. God's promise to the newly named Abraham and Sarah was profound and compassionate: they were to be, respectively, the father of a multitude and a princess free of all hint of distress. The question was whether they were able to accept this gift of new identity in God or whether their sights were still stuck on their future reward.

This does, however, knock down to size the waiting of Advent—four weeks seems as nothing next to twenty-six years. At the same time it speaks a powerful word of comfort to those whose waiting has stretched on and on. Resolution may not be as we expect it to be, nor even as swift as we hope. Sometimes it may not come at all, but God's presence and promise remain now, even if the future is uncertain.

". . . your wife Sarah shall have a son . . ."
And Sarah was listening at the tent entrance
behind him. Now Abraham and Sarah were old,
advanced in age; it had ceased to be with Sarah
after the manner of women. So Sarah laughed to
herself, saying, "After I have grown old, and my
husband is old, shall I have pleasure?"

GENESIS 18:10–12

FOR FURTHER READING
Genesis 18:1–15

I've never quite grown out of a tendency to want to laugh at the most inappropriate of moments. I feel a bubble starting somewhere around my feet and rising, slowly and inexorably, upward. The more I fight it, the quicker it rises. The only thing that has changed as I've gotten older is that I'm now more skilled in hiding it than I was. As a result, I relate entirely to Sarah's spontaneous guffaw of laughter, and commiserate with her that, though she allowed it to spill out, she did so inside the tent where it shouldn't have been heard had it not been that one of her visitors was God.

That laugh haunts me because beneath it lies a maelstrom of emotions. First and foremost, it expresses the utter ridiculousness of the promise: "That was a joke wasn't it? I'm a barren old woman, what a ridiculous idea."

Alongside this, however, is a tinge of bitterness and cynicism: "Yeh, yeh, you promised that last time, oh and the time before, and yes the time before that too. Don't expect me to fall for that one again."

But woven into this is also a strand of yearning: "Abraham and I are now too old; we can't expect that kind of pleasure at our age . . . can we? There was a time for such pleasure, and we missed it, surely it is now too late?"

This laugh laced with hilarity, cynicism, and wistfulness burst out of Sarah, and God, who hears everything, heard and understood all the pain and sense of betrayal behind her guffaw and assures her of the reality of the promise.

What is interesting is Sarah's reaction at this point. The burst of laughter was a moment of genuine, deeply held emotion but, the moment it was recognized as such, she backed down and claimed that it didn't happen . . . because she was afraid. The Greek translation of the Hebrew text translates this as "she was afraid for," exactly the same construction as the ending of Mark's Gospel, "they . . . fled . . . for they were afraid" (Mark 16:8). Now on one level this construction is unremarkable. If, in Greek, one wanted to have a two-word sentence including the word *for*, then the only place to put it is second; it cannot go in any other place. Nevertheless, the brevity of the sentence leads to a certain clunky style which draws our attention to it. The parallels between the two accounts are striking. Sarah has been waiting and waiting for the fulfillment of the promise, and when its fulfillment approached, fear overtook, and she found herself unable to accept either the promise (she laughed) or God's compassionate recognition of her reaction to it. In a similar way, the women at the tomb had been waiting and waiting for the fulfillment of God's promise of salvation; the thing that they wanted above all was for Jesus not to be dead, yet in the face of the news about his resurrection they fled because of their fear.

It is a part of human nature that we often find it as hard to deal with the fulfillment of things for which we have yearned, as for the things we want but never get. Would it have been different if they had waited in the present moment in the presence of God? Would they then have been able to cope with the fulfillment better if they were prepared and ready for God's intervention? It is far too simplistic to assume that they would. Both Sarah and the women at the tomb reacted out of a genuine, deeply held emotion, and they were right to do so, but God's response to Sarah is intriguing. God didn't reprimand her for her fear but refused to allow her to hide behind a pretense that masked her true feelings, reminding her that she did, in fact, laugh ("Oh yes, you did laugh," 18:15). This returns us one more time to God's desire to accompany us on the way; all that is asked of us is that we are honest about how we feel, so that we can accept God's word of assurance: "At the set time, I will return to you. . . ." (Genesis 18:14).

There is, of course, a wonderful ending to this story which we read in Genesis 21. Sarah did bear a son and she called him "laughter," for that is what Isaac means in Hebrew. God took her irony, her bitterness, and her longing and transformed it into a sound of pure joy, as Sarah says in Genesis 21:6: "God has brought laughter for me; everyone who hears will laugh with me." Sarah is no longer a despised, disappointed old woman but a spring of joy whose laughter is so infectious that it will bring joy to all her friends.

The story of Sarah's laughter speaks profoundly of the nature of God. God yearns to receive our cynical, wistful laughter and to transform it into shouts of pure joy. The God who creates and recreates, who brings to life and revives, is the kind of God who yearns to breathe new life into the depth of our emotions, asking that we own those moments of cynical but genuine emotion ("Oh yes, you did laugh," Genesis 18:15) so that they can be transformed into infectious peals of joyful laughter.

"Take your son, your only son Isaac,
whom you love, and go to the land of Moriah,
and offer him there as a burnt-offering
on one of the mountains that I shall tell you."

GENESIS 22:2

FOR FURTHER READING
Genesis 22:1–19

My father is a particularly gifted preacher to people who live in a non-book culture. His sermons have always been highly visual, involved many illustrations and quite a lot of dressing up. Many people have been deeply moved by his preaching, but one particular sermon is seared into my memory. I was about ten and the passage for the sermon was Genesis 22 and the sacrifice of Isaac. This sermon involved a part for me (as I have no brothers) and there are no prizes for guessing that was the part of Isaac. I was duly laid on a table for an altar and my dad held a knife up as though to kill me. I am sure that the rest of the congregation found it a very helpful illustration, but I have hated the story ever since.

The sermon achieved its aim. I came to grips with the story, with its dark undercurrents, in a way I might never otherwise have done and realized what this meant for Isaac. Though this passage is normally held up as yet another example of Abraham's faithfulness, I am implacably on Isaac's side. Why did he have to go through this to prove the faithfulness of his father and the clemency of God? As I have studied this more closely, I have realized that I am not the only one to ask questions about this passage.

In Jewish tradition this story is known as the "Aqedah," which is simply the Hebrew word for *binding*. There are many traditions associated with the Aqedah, but one of them includes a tradition in which Isaac talks to Ishmael and argues that he offered himself as a sacrifice at the age of thirty-seven in full knowledge of what he was doing. A similar tradition exists in the Qur'an, though this time concerning Ishmael rather than Isaac. Here Abraham shares God's command to sacrifice Ishmael with his son, and Ishmael agrees that they should do what God wants. Both of these traditions indicate that the son, whether Isaac or Ishmael, is involved in the decision, evidently because that makes the story much easier to accept.

Of course, it is important to bear in mind that Genesis 22 is told solely from Abraham's point of view. God's command to Abraham, and Abraham's interpretation of that command, are all told from Abraham's perspective. We know nothing of why God commanded him to act like this, what he actually said or whether Isaac had heard from God anything about what was to happen. It is a story involving three characters, or indeed four if we include Sarah, but we hear only one side of the tale. The other three sides—those of God, Isaac, and Sarah—may have had a very different tale to tell.

Another interpretation of this story is that it is included as a means of illustrating that God, in fact, did not approve of child sacrifice (unlike some of the other cultures around in which it played an important part) and that the real point of this story was to show that God did not approve of such actions. This is a nice thought but smacks a little of desperation. There is nothing in the text to indicate that this is what was meant, nor indeed that child sacrifice was common before Abraham's time.

We are left, then, with the dark mystery of God. There are times in the Bible when God appears to act in a simply incomprehensible way. On those occasions we are faced with a range of options:

- Ignore the story and hope we don't have to think about it too often (a popular option for many!).

- Focus on the good side of the story (that it shows Abraham's faithfulness and God's mercy) and assume that the rest was culturally conditioned.

- Find explanations that make God's actions more palatable (that Isaac knew and agreed to the sacrifice).

- Remain with the dark side of the story and wrestle with it.

The final solution—that of wrestling with the tradition—is my own preferred option. I often think that the story of Jacob who wrestled with the angel until morning, and then walked away wounded but blessed (Genesis 32:22–32), is a good metaphor for biblical interpretation. If we take the easier route, we domesticate God into the kind of God that we would be, or would like God to be. The truth, however, is that God is not the kind of God we would be, nor indeed, always, the kind we like. But God is God and sees the created, beloved world in its entirety. The Bible presents an image of God that is not always to our liking, so we have to wrestle with it, to struggle—and sometimes to shout and scream about it. When this happens, we inevitably walk away *wounded* in the sense that we are not the people we were when we began. We may still hate the story, but we have allowed it to alter us in some way or another. One thing that reading the Bible, and in particular the Hebrew Scriptures, tells us, is that God doesn't mind us arguing (at the end of Genesis 18 Abraham famously argued with God about the destruction of Sodom) but does ask us to engage. Politely pretending that God is not like that, is, in my view, the last thing that God would want.

The effect of this odd command to Abraham is that, one more time, God appears to put his promise in jeopardy. At last we have an heir from which the multitude of Abraham's descendants can descend, but then God appears to want to start all over again. Yet one more time God appears to be saying that it is not the goal that is the important thing, but the journey along the way and the one with whom we travel.

CLOSING REFLECTIONS

The story of Abraham and Sarah is a story of waiting *par excellence*. The promise that first summoned them from their home, as described at the start of this chapter, remains unfulfilled at the end. Abraham's descendants are not yet multitudes, and the following episodes of the story show how, when they become multitudes at last in Egypt, they no longer have the land. God's promise to Abraham wobbles on precariously until at last, under Joshua, the *multitudes* settle in the *land*, though then we are left to worry about whether their relationship with God is all that it might be.

The theme that bubbles along throughout the Hebrew Scriptures is the question of the goal of God's promise. For Abraham, it is an heir, for Moses, it is the land, but very quickly it becomes whether God will make them a great nation rather than a downtrodden, oppressed one. Throughout this story we encounter a God who stands by, pleading with the people to stop and realize that the goal is not, in fact, the most important thing. Much more important than the goal is the presence of God: walking with us on the way and helping us to realize that waiting can be as important as achieving.

Abraham and Sarah become symbols for us not only of faith but also of waiting: of waiting as an essential part of our journey with God, of waiting being vital for the proper unfolding of God's plan, and of waiting being as important as that for which we wait. God summons us to go out but does not always tell us where to, or why . . . for that we must wait, but in the waiting we can, sometimes, discover a meaning.

▦

TWO

WAITING FOR THE DAY OF THE LORD

The Prophets

INTRODUCTION

The second candle on the Advent wreath is associated with the prophets and, in particular, their prophecies of the "one who is to come." With this candle, therefore, we are waiting for the future and all that it might hold. As soon as we say this, however, it becomes clear that we have to ask a fundamental question: which precise future?

▪ The prophets' future that may or may not have come to fruition before the time of Jesus.

▪ Israel's future that came to fruition at the time of Jesus.

▪ Our own future that will come to fruition at the end of all times (as well as partially during our lifetimes).

Confused? You should be, because of course the answer to each of these questions is yes and no. Yes because each one of these futures is awaited and anticipated during Advent, and no because any one of these awaited futures is incomplete without the others. In order to explain prophetic fulfillment, the metaphor of a telescope is often used. You can look through a telescope when it is closed up and see a nearer scene, or you can open it halfway and see a scene slightly further off, or you can extend it to its full extent and see far into the distance. In a way, the prophetic prophecies are like this: true in their own situation but also in Jesus'; true in Jesus' but also in ours; true in ours but also at the end times with the obvious proviso that they were never more true than at the time of Jesus. If it is possible for something to be more and less true, then they are fully and entirely true only of Jesus and probably also of the end times; at other times are partially, fragmentarily true, still true but in not so much depth or breadth.

We are left, though, with the question, "What is it that we are waiting for?" This is something that will unfold as we explore each prophecy in turn. The choice of prophetic passages that could be used here is extensive. Consequently, we shall look at those most closely associated with waiting for Christmas. The passages chosen come partially from the lectionary for Advent and partially from the Service of Nine Lessons and Carols, which begins by looking forward, through the Hebrew Scriptures to the birth of Christ.

*The virgin will be with child and will give birth
to a son, and will call him Immanuel.
He will eat curds and honey when he knows
enough to reject the wrong and choose the right.
But before the boy knows enough to reject the
wrong and choose the right, . . . the land of the
two kings you dread will be laid waste.*

ISAIAH 7:14–16 NIV

FOR FURTHER READING
Isaiah 7:1–17

This is surely one of the most iconic prophecies used of the birth of Jesus. I only have to hear these words and I recall the smell of candle wax mingled with fir trees, hear the hum of "Once in Royal David's City," and feel a tingle of excitement. This prophecy lies right at the heart of Christmas and is picked up in Matthew's Gospel ("'The virgin will be with child and will give birth to a son, and they will call him Immanuel'—which means, 'God with us,'" 1:23 NIV) as a prophecy of Jesus' birth. You don't have to read very far in this prophecy, however, before the feeling of Christmas disintegrates. What on earth has the laying to waste of the land of two kings got to do with Christmas? Well nothing at all, and this is where we become alerted to the fact that this prophecy speaks into at least two (if not more) contexts.

Isaiah's prophecy here addresses a very specific context in the history of Judah, and most unusually within the Hebrew Scriptures it is possible to date this prophecy with a fair degree of certainty. In ca. 735–733 BC Judah was plunged into crisis by her neighbors. For a considerable period Judah, along with most other countries in the region, had been under the control of the great Assyrian army. Around this time, however, both Israel (the northern kingdom) and Syria decided to rebel against their Assyrian conquerors. In order to do this, they attempted to press Judah into an alliance with them to strengthen the rebellion. When Judah declined, Israel and Syria decided to invade Judah to force their compliance, so they fought against Judah with the intention of overthrowing Ahaz, who was king of Judah at the time, and replacing him with the son of Tabeel (Isaiah 7:1–9).

Isaiah, with his son Shear-jashub, was sent out to meet Ahaz "at the end of the conduit of the upper pool" (7:3) to offer him words of reassurance: that, if he remained steadfast, God would save him. In the context of this, Isaiah gave Ahaz a sign of God's trustworthiness—despite Ahaz's reluctance to accept it—which was that a young woman would conceive, bear a son, and call him Immanuel and that before he knew the difference between right and wrong the land of the two kings of Israel and Syria would be laid waste.

The original prophecy, therefore, was simply about timing. In the amount of time it takes for a woman to conceive, bear a son, and bring him up to know the difference between wrong and right, this situation that caused Ahaz such stress would be resolved. An important postscript to this story is that Ahaz did not, in fact, do what God commanded. He did not remain steadfast and instead sent off to Assyria for help, an action that may have contributed to the utter destruction of the northern kingdom of Israel a few years later in 722 BC.

So what has this to do with Christmas? At first glance, not a lot; the theories about how best to interpret this passage, and whether it can be used at Christmas are endless. One of the most important of these debates is over the word for young woman/virgin in verse 14. In Hebrew the word *almah* means simply "a young girl of marriageable age," who has reached the age of fertility; the Greek translators of the Hebrew, however, chose to translate this with the word *parthenos*, that as well as meaning young woman also means virgin. In other words, they narrowed the meaning of the word. In Hebrew it is simply a description of age; in Greek it is a specific description of a girl who is of marriageable age but not yet married. It has been argued that therefore the whole tradition of the virgin birth has been based on a mistranslation of Hebrew into Greek and furthermore shows that the whole story is a fabrication based upon this mistranslation.

In my opinion, this is to miss the point of what Matthew is doing here. This is a prophecy about God's imminent salvation of the people of God. The message is clear: once this child is born you should be on the lookout for salvation as it will only be a matter of time before God's salvation breaks on the world. Matthew seems to be using this as a pledge for the future: once you see this event taking place, you will know that salvation is near.

The virginity—or not—of the young woman is not as important as it has been made to be in many discussions. The point of the prophecy is not so much about virginity as it is about salvation.

Nevertheless, Matthew sees this prophecy fulfilled in Jesus in a way that has never been done before; the fact that this involves a dimension of fulfillment through the virginity of Jesus' conception that has not been evident previously, simply demonstrates the impact of its fulfillment. It would be a shame, however, to miss the resounding proclamation of salvation while we argue over whether Matthew is allowed to use the prophecy like this.

This first prophecy alerts us to the kind of waiting associated with this candle of Advent. Prophetic waiting looks eagerly for signs of God's salvation in our midst; it looks backward remembering God's glorious salvation in the past; forward to the time in the future when it will break forth again; and all around us for signs of its presence now. Just as Isaiah's original sign was designed to make Ahaz alert to God's salvation, so Matthew's appropriation of the prophecy is intended to remind his readers to look and look for Immanuel, "God with us," past, present, and future. The season of Advent reminds us to continue the search for God's presence today, alert as ever for signs of God's salvation.

For a child has been born for us, a son given to us; authority rests upon his shoulders; and he is named Wonderful Counsellor, Mighty God, Everlasting Father, Prince of Peace. His authority shall grow continually, and there shall be endless peace for the throne of David and his kingdom. He will establish and uphold it with justice and with righteousness from this time onward and forevermore.

ISAIAH 9:6–7

FOR FURTHER READING
Isaiah 9:1–7

This passage of Isaiah has been famously set to music by Handel in his oratorio *Messiah*. Those who know the piece well may already be humming to themselves: "For unto us a child is born, unto us a son is given. . . ." Handel's use of this prophecy introduces us to a different kind of messianic prophecy from the one in Isaiah 7:14. The link between Isaiah 7:14 and Jesus is made for us by Matthew; the link between Isaiah 9:6–7 and Jesus is made by Christian tradition (Handel isn't the only one to make the connection) on the grounds of its content, and its content here does seem an ideal description of Jesus and all that he will do.

One of the important features to notice about this passage, however, is that it seems totally out of place at this point in Isaiah. If you read around this passage you will notice Isaiah's overwhelming message of gloom and disaster. Chapter 8 talks of how God's people in Judah are going to be overwhelmed by their enemy and that many are going to stumble and be destroyed. Chapter 9 reminds them of the disaster that has already fallen on Israel (their neighbors in the northern kingdom). Between these terrible prophecies sits 9:1–7, which is a beam of light in a gloomy territory.

Somewhat inevitably, this has caused scholars to attempt to work out why it is here: has it been inserted at a later date, perhaps by someone who is not Isaiah? Does it refer to a small group of people in Judah who will escape the coming disaster? Thankfully, since no consensus has yet been achieved on this, it is not our task to decide that here, but what this does do is highlight the light and shade that exist at this point in Isaiah. For obvious reasons, the prophecies from Isaiah that we use around Christmas time are the cheery ones: the ones that talk about light, hope, and God's salvation. It is easy to forget, then, that prophets like Isaiah prophesied more about gloom than about hope; more about disaster than about salvation. One of the factors with which the recipients of these prophecies struggled was the prophetic reinterpretation of what the "day of the Lord" was going to look like.

There was widespread hope of God's intervention in the world—a "day of the Lord"—in which God would drive out Israel and Judah's enemies and all would be peaceful once more. The message of many prophets, like Amos, was that the day of the Lord was going to be the opposite of what they expected: suffering, punishment, and bloodshed rather than reward, joy, and hope. In Isaiah, however, we find a mix of the two: disaster with the odd fragment of peace; gloom with a gleam of light; despair with a glimmer of hope. In Isaiah they seem to go hand in hand. This passage is an example of a hopeful prophecy, but it has to be read alongside the less cheerful prophecies to get a proper sense of the light and shade of the first part of the book.

So what is Isaiah's message? Disaster or peace? Despair or hope? It is hard to tell whether Isaiah sees the coming catastrophe as laced with hope or whether he sees it coming after the catastrophe, though his statement in verse 2 ("The people who walked in darkness have seen a great light . . . on them light has shined") suggests that the light is shining in the gloom. Nevertheless, a tradition certainly existed, influenced by traditions like this, that saw future hope as dawning beyond the current situation of despair. This tradition became so important that it appears that at the time of Jesus, many people actively looked forward to the time when the current time of despair would be swept away and a new era of peace and prosperity would dawn. What the disciples struggled to understand about Jesus was that he had not come to drive away the old, but as a light to shine into the world as it was.

This world is a world of light *and* shade; not just light or just shade. Isaiah knew that the disaster awaiting Judah—a disaster largely of their own making—had to be faced in the knowledge that woven into it and beyond it were signs of hope; so also Jesus calls us to face the grim realities of the world in which we live—grim realities again often of our own making—but again in the knowledge that woven into this world is the light of Jesus. Jesus does bring the peace, established with justice and upheld with righteousness, that Isaiah prophesied, but it was and is a peace in the midst of conflict.

As is so often the case, Jesus fulfils these ancient prophecies in a surprising way, and it is through weaving light into the shade of our present world that he evokes wonder by the wisdom of his counsel (wonderful counsellor); shows the power of God in the world (mighty God); cares eternally just like a parent (everlasting father); and is the source of all well-being for God's people (prince of peace). Jesus lived as wonderful counsellor, mighty God, everlasting father, and prince of peace in the midst of our broken, despairing world, shining in the darkness and bringing hope.

It is this light shining in the darkness for which we wait, and the season of Advent calls us to readjust our eyes in that darkness so that we can see glimmers of the Light of the World, glowing and pointing us forward to that ultimate time in the future when everything will be fulfilled and, in the words of John Donne's prayer "Bring us, O Lord, at our last awakening," "there will be no darkness or dazzling but one equal light."

*The wolf shall live with the lamb, the leopard
shall lie down with the kid, the calf and the lion and
the fatling together, and a little child shall
lead them. The cow and the bear shall graze,
their young shall lie down together; and the lion
shall eat straw like the ox. The nursing child shall
play over the hole of the asp, and the weaned child
shall put its hand on the adder's den. They will not
hurt or destroy on all my holy mountain;
for the earth will be full of the knowledge of the
LORD as the waters cover the sea.*

ISAIAH 11:6-9

FOR FURTHER READING
Isaiah 11:1-9

I wonder what Richard Attenborough would
make of this prophecy? The image evokes a zoo of a
fantastical kind, where no enclosures are necessary,
because the wild animals (and indeed the humans) are
no longer dangerous. The fierce animals of prey—the
wolves, leopards, lions, and bears—will frolic, sleep,
and eat *with* their prey—the lamb, the kid, the calf, the
fatling (a word used for any animal suitable for sacrifice),
child, cow, and ox—rather than eating *them* as they

usually would. Forget your visit to the zoo where you watched a lion gorging on a hunk of meat, or the TV programs about the natural world when you watched the sadly inevitable death of a beautiful gazelle leaping across the plain. This is a vision of some kind of return to the Garden of Eden (that assumes that the animals didn't eat each other there either), when the world will be so suffused with peace that even the natural world will eschew their gory pastimes. This vision is very clearly a vision of the far distant future, of a time way beyond the nearer catastrophe to come, and raises for us that other important theme, that Advent raises, that is what we might call "the end of the world."

A few words on that before we turn our attention to what it means for Advent-waiting. One of the problems of calling the event "the end of the world" is that it implies an ultimate finality; that after the end it is gone . . . no more world. There is, I believe a bumper sticker in the United States that reads: "In case of the rapture . . . this car will have no driver"; the assumption being that somehow the lives of the faithful will then be lived elsewhere, in heaven. This is not in line with the many biblical visions of a climactic event in the future when God intervenes in the world. Even the book of Revelation, which portrays the "end," also describes a "beginning"; the new heaven *and* the new earth descend ready for occupation. There seems no doubt that there would, in fact, be an earthly place for bears to graze alongside cows, and for wolves to gambol with the lambs, unlikely as that may seem. If Isaiah's prophecy is to be located in this far, far off location beyond "the end," then there must still be a world to inhabit, however different from our own.

When Jesus ascended into heaven, the disciples were left gazing upward openmouthed, wondering where he had gone. The image of the end of the world rather encourages Christians to continue standing around with similarly vacant expressions on our faces waiting for the end to come. This does not seem to be the intention of passages such as this one in Isaiah, nor is it intended to make us feel doubly bad about the state of the world now. Here on the one hand is the promise of a lion playing fol-low-the-leader with a child and a calf; there on the other is a lion doing what lions do now—killing said child and calf for its dinner. Visions of the end exist neither so that we all stand around training our eyes on the horizon and waiting, nor so that we can feel depressed about the state of our current world as it is, but so that we can learn to recognize signs of that new reality and to encourage their birth in our midst now. Visions of the end show us more of the world as God yearns for it to be when all things will come to fulfillment, and to remind us that we can see flashes of that end time in our world now.

This is not to encourage us all to rush off and open wild beast training academies in which leopards are trained to curl up with goats—without taking a quick snack—but to encourage us to look out for and celebrate those times in our world when something like this happens: when white South Africans, for example, finally began to recognize black South Africans as their brothers and sisters; when, in Northern Ireland, Sinn Fein and the Democratic Unionist Party agreed to share power; when a mother whose child was killed forgave the killers rather than seeking revenge; when in your own life you have been able to forgive someone who has hurt you rather than give vent to your anger. These are all end-time moments, breaking into our world now.

Visions of a glorious future, such as this one in Isaiah 11, stir us into waiting but also into action. Waiting for the end times challenges us to bring about more and more of these end-time moments, and Advent is a time when we are called to reflect on where such moments might lie in our own lives, our own communities, and our own world, and also to renew our determination to bring about such world-shattering peace wherever God wills it to be.

*But you, O Bethlehem of Ephrathah, who are one
of the little clans of Judah, from you shall come
forth for me one who is to rule in Israel, whose
origin is from of old, from ancient days.*

MICAH 5:2

FOR FURTHER READING
Micah 5:2–5a

I don't know about you, but I hate getting this passage
to read out loud. Many people dread getting those readings with the complex Hebrew and Greek names in them,
but Ephrathah produces a particular challenge, not of
knowing *how* to pronounce it but of *being able* to do
so with panache . . . and without spitting. If it is any
comfort, the word isn't even essential to the passage. In
Genesis 48:7 Ephrathah is identified as the place near
which Rachel was buried and seems to be simply another
name for Bethelehem, so probably not Bethlehem *of*
Ephrathah but Bethlehem, Ephrathah, two names for
the same place; it is used in a similar way in Ruth 4:11
("May you produce children in Ephrathah and bestow
a name in Bethlehem"), a wish not entirely unconnected
to this prophecy as of course Ruth and Boaz's son was
Obed, who was King David's grandfather.

The context of Micah's prophecy is very similar to that of the prophecies from the early part of Isaiah that we explored above. Micah prophesied to Judah, the southern kingdom, in the reigns of Jotham (742–735 BC), Ahaz (735–715 BC) and Hezekiah (715–687 BC), though it is unlikely that he began at the beginning of Jotham's reign and ended at the end of Hezekiah's. Thus, the major part of his prophecy covers Ahaz's reign just as Isaiah's did, so they may well have been prophesying at the same time. The greatest part of Micah's prophecy was aimed at the wealthy living in Jerusalem, who oppressed the poor by their pursuit of riches.

In the context of this, Micah's prophecy, that for us evokes a hopeful Christmas message, was in fact a powerful condemnation of the king. The first verse of chapter 5, for good reason, is not included in the popular Christmas reading of this passage; the good reason is that it is not entirely clear what it means. The difference between the NRSV and TNIV (Today's New International Version) illustrates how hard translators find it to translate this verse:

NRSV: "Now you are walled around with a wall."
TNIV: "Marshal your troops now."

A brief glance at the Hebrew makes it clear what the problem is. The Hebrew word translated "walled around" in the NRSV and "marshal" in the TNIV can mean, in the form it takes here, either to cut yourself as in a religious frenzy or to throng around. One commentator has suggested that it means that the inhabitants of Jerusalem have been slashing themselves as in a religious frenzy in the hope of being saved from their enemies.

Whatever the correct translation of verse 1, verse 2 makes it clear that the current situation will only be solved with a clean slate. Since the time of David and the Davidic dynasty, the kings have been born in Jerusalem, in the royal palace. Micah's prophecy indicates that he believes that the only hope for the future is to go back to the beginning and try again. The reference to Bethlehem is, of course, a reference to David's place of birth, so Micah's prophecy maintains that the hope for the future lies in a king *like* David but not from the Davidic line that is currently in Jerusalem.

What seems to have happened is that the ruling elite, including the kings, have become so self-satisfied that they no longer care for anyone apart from themselves. The only solution, then, is to return to the humble roots of King David. The word that Micah uses to describe Bethlehem literally means "insignificant" or "youngest" and seems to be a deliberate reference to David, who was himself the most insignificant and youngest of his brothers. True kingship, Micah seems to be saying, lies in the humble, insignificant roots of David, not in the arrogant, power hungry courts of the king.

It is no wonder that King Herod the Great is so rattled by being reminded of this prophecy at the time of Jesus

(Matthew 2:3–6). Herod had very little claim to kingship in the first place and had achieved the position he had by clever use of power and manipulation of his links with the Romans. He was paranoid about other people taking his power and killed many people, including members of his own family, when he feared they were gaining too much power. The reminder that true kingship lay in the opposite of all he stood for would have been deeply unwelcome.

The knowledge of this makes this prophecy even more applicable to Jesus. Jesus follows David in his origins in the most insignificant tribe of Israel and, by his life and actions, shows that true kingship is to be found in humility, and that the accumulation of great wealth and power do nothing to shore up a crumbling claim to kingship. Herod, like the kings of Micah's day, must demonstrate the veracity of their kingship by acting justly, by steadfast love, and by walking humbly with God (Micah 6:8).

Given the importance—and the appropriateness of its application to Jesus—of the use of the word "insignificant" for Bethlehem, it is odd that Matthew has reversed the idea in his quotation and said that Bethlehem is "by no means least" among the rulers of Judah. Probably the best explanation of this is that Matthew, being all too aware of Bethlehem's low status, is reminding people that it might be insignificant, but it is the birthplace of two great kings: first David and now

Jesus. In true gospel fashion the first (Jerusalem) will be last, and the last (Bethlehem) first.

This prophecy is not so much a romantic reminder of the special place of Bethlehem in God's plan, as it is a radical proclamation of the unsettling truth of God's plan for the world; a plan that insists on justice, steadfast love, and on walking with God in humility. Both Micah and Matthew were issuing a disturbing message to the rulers of their day: God's power does not rest on wealth but on justice, not on wielding power but on steadfast love. It was never a popular message and, I suspect, remains as unpopular today as it ever was.

And I will save the lame and gather the outcast, and I will change their shame into praise and renown in all the earth.

ZEPHANIAH 3:19

FOR FURTHER READING
Zephaniah 3:14–20

I have never actually seen the Monty Python "Four Yorkshire Men" sketch, but its popularity was such that, when I was growing up, my friends would act out bits of it. The essence of the sketch was that four

Yorkshire men were vying for the dubious position of being recognized as having had the worst childhood (for example, "We lived for three months in a paper bag in a septic tank . . ." "Luxury, we used to . . ."). There is something quintessentially British about competing over who was the most poor, most deprived, and had the worst childhood, and this is what this sketch tapped into. Even today when standards of living are much higher, very few people feel "rich." An apocryphal story asks in a survey how much money would be enough for people, to which the response is "a little bit more."

That attitude skews our response to passages like this, or the one in Isaiah 61:1, that is also used around Advent time ("He has sent me to bring good news to the oppressed, to bind up the brokenhearted, to proclaim liberty to the captives, and release to the prisoners"), notably read by Jesus in Luke 4:18. In both of these passages God's particular promise to the poor and lame for refuge, freedom, and healing is announced, and it is so easy to interpret these passages solely in terms of ourselves and the ways in which we are poor and oppressed.

Of course, these prophecies, in their original context, were meant generally. The book of Zephaniah is set in the seventh century BC (about a century later than the eighth-century prophecies from Isaiah that we looked at earlier) during the reign of Josiah and prophesies a time when disaster will strike the land of Judah. This prophecy is a rare note of hope in a prophecy of doom, when Zephaniah promises a future time when all will be well. In this context, the saving of the lame and the gathering of the outcast would have had general reference because, having suffered such devastation, so many would have been lame and cast out. Zephaniah's message of hope spoke generally to a society in need of comfort.

Jesus' application of this prophecy, however, seems to shift its focus. One of the great challenges of Jesus' ministry was, and is, the call to recognize that prophecies like this are not about us, or at least not entirely about us. Jesus, as he made clear in the synagogue as described in Luke 4, understood his calling to be a perfect fulfilment of this prophecy through his care for the lame and oppressed of his day. Those who lived during the time of Jesus had genuine grounds to feel that they fit into these categories: the rule of the Roman Empire was deeply resented, and there were many in financial hardship because of the taxation system. Jesus does not, however, seem to interpret this prophecy in terms of the whole people of God, but in terms of those who were pushed to the very edge of the society of his day.

The blind, the lame, the deaf, the demon possessed, those hemorrhaging blood, and so on, are easily understood as the recipients of this prophecy, because, due to the purity regulations within the temple, they were unable to enter the main temple precincts and to take part in the sacrificial worship that made up the very heart of life as a Jew. Tax collectors and prostitutes are, perhaps, a little more surprising, though they have one important feature in common. Both tax collectors and prostitutes had relationships with the hated Roman occupying force: the tax collectors because their role was to collect the Roman taxes on behalf of the emperor, and the prostitutes because that was where their major revenue was to be found. They were widely hated because they were perceived to have made choices that put them in this relationship with the Romans, and thereby rendered themselves permanently on the outskirts of society.

Jesus chose to interpret this message of salvation in terms of those who, whether by circumstance or choice, were outcasts in society. Somewhat surprisingly, he did not choose people like the dispossessed Galilean farmers, forced to live in the hills away from their land because of a lack of money and who were to a certain extent admired by those they left behind. Jesus chose to gather in as part of the outcasts, people who were despised and vilified by the society in which they lived, and it was this that made so many people struggle to understand him. Why interpret this prophecy in this way? Surely there were many more acceptable "outcasts" that he could have ministered to?

Jesus' challenge remains as hard today as it was then. We are, of course, right to recognize that the God who saves the lame and gathers in the outcasts will do the same for us: all the ways in which we are lame and outcast *are* and *will be* redeemed in Christ Jesus; but this does not mean that we have the monopoly on "lameness" and "outcast-ness." Jesus still seeks out those who are right on the edge of society; those who we despise and vilify . . . and most challenging of all calls us to do the same.

Comfort, O comfort my people, says your God.
Speak tenderly to Jerusalem, and cry to her that
she has served her term, that her penalty is paid,
that she has received from the LORD's *hand*
double for all her sins.

ISAIAH 40:1–2

■

FOR FURTHER READING
Isaiah 40:1–11

When I was a child there was a song sung quite regularly in church that began "Comfort ye, comfort ye my people," drawn from Isaiah 40. In the way that children do, because those words didn't make immediate sense to me, I translated them into words that did, and I was convinced they meant "Come for tea, come for tea my people." I had a mental image of God, sitting in a comfortable chair with a huge teapot, inviting everyone in for a cup of tea. I still feel a twinge of disappointment that these were not the words Isaiah originally intended.

Nevertheless, Isaiah's message of hope here rings out a loud message of comfort. Coming after the previous three passages we have explored from Isaiah, its tone has changed completely. From now on in Isaiah the message is more comfort than catastrophe, more hope than despair. In fact, it seems as though it is written into an entirely different context from the prophecies that can be found in Isaiah 1–39, to the extent that most scholars would argue that the context for this passage is not the eighth century BC but the sixth century BC. The people have, at last, been conquered by their overlords (though in the end it was the Babylonians and not the Assyrians who destroyed them) and taken away into exile in Babylon. This message seems to come at the end of that period, when they are about to be released and sent back home again. Once the exile has happened, God issues comfort to the people and prepares them, not only for their own return home, but for God's return as well ("In the wilderness prepare the way of the Lord," 40:3).

This message is the opposite of Ezekiel's. At the start of the exilic period Ezekiel prophesied strikingly, if a little weirdly for some people's tastes, about his vision of God's chariot (see, for example, Ezekiel 1), which eventually in chapter 11 became God's transport out of the temple and away from the city. The place where God dwelt in the midst of the people was now deserted. In a very odd kind of way this abandonment was a message of comfort: the temple was destroyed by the Babylonians, but if God was no longer in it, God was not destroyed. Isaiah 40, then, proclaims the other side of Ezekiel's message: the time of abandonment has come to an end and a way must be prepared for God's return.

One of the features of this passage that cannot be communicated in modern English is that the ringing, opening cry "Comfort, O comfort my people" is a plural command and not a singular one. God is not here telling his prophet to go and comfort his people. Instead, the cry goes out, "Is there anyone out there who will comfort my people?" This whole passage begins with God searching for people to bring comfort and, not only that, also to speak "to the heart of Jerusalem" (which is a more literal translation of the Hebrew than "speak tenderly to Jerusalem"). The NRSV translation doesn't quite capture the whole meaning here. Of course the message will be tender, but the point is that the message spoken must speak to the very heart of the people; it will comfort their brokenness but also resonate truthfully, deep within them. Jerusalem—the place where God dwelt among the people—is to take comfort because God will return.

One of the fascinating features of this passage is the number of voices who speak in it:

- We begin with God in verse 1,

- continue with another unnamed voice in verse 3,

- and another (or the same one?) in verse 6,

- then "I" speaks in verse 6 (this "I" is presumably the prophet),

- and finally Zion/Jerusalem is commanded to speak in verse 9.

The image is a little like passing on a baton in a relay race. God calls a message of comfort, and voice after voice picks it up, until at last Jerusalem itself is commanded to speak it. What is remarkable about this is that Jerusalem, the recipient of the message of comfort, becomes the means for passing it on throughout the whole of Judah. Jerusalem, itself, is to be transformed from a broken, bruised city of mourning into one that vibrantly proclaims God's presence: the message that Jerusalem is to proclaim is "See, the Lord God is coming."

There seems to be something important about this. Comfort here, then, is not about passively receiving a message of tenderness but about transformation that arises from a deep recognition of truth. Once the people of Jerusalem can recognize that God really is coming back, then they become the means by which this message is proclaimed. They must go to a high mountain and shout it out loudly so that it is passed on to all the cities of Judah who are also in dire need of comfort. Anyone who has taught knows that there is nothing like having to teach a subject to make you realize that you understand it (or not!). Jerusalem's proclamation of God's return requires its people not just to receive the message of comfort, but to comprehend it and make it their own so that they, in their turn, can proclaim it to others.

Jerusalem was called, in this passage, to a very active form of waiting: the people must hear the message, grasp it, make it their own, and pass it on. The comfort, then, is passed on in a chain and is not left in a cul-de-sac; it is sent forward and not kept just for themselves. The waiting, to which we are called in Advent, is a similar kind of waiting in which we hear and receive the message of God's presence and are transformed by it, so that we in our turn can pass it on.

CLOSING REFLECTIONS

During Advent we are called to observe, and indeed join in with, the collapsing of time. Prophecies into situations in the eighth century BC become revived and renewed in the first century; prophecies appropriately applied in the first century are relevant again in the twenty-first century. So, for example, a prophecy such as Isaiah 7:14–16, designed to be a beam of hope, of God with us, in the eighth century BC was picked up and perfectly fulfilled in Jesus; that same prophecy can also be a beam of hope, of God with us today. In the same way, God's message of reassuring comfort designed to be heard and proclaimed by the exiles, still rings in our ears over 2,500 years later. At the same time, hope that is based on what will happen at the end of time becomes relevant today, as well as 2,000 years ago. Past collapses into present, present into future, future into the past, and so on.

Advent invites us to inhabit a swirl of time that stretches forward and backward but by doing so anchors us in the present. It is by living in this collapsing, swirling time that God reminds us of what is important about our lives now. At the start of this chapter I asked what we are waiting for and the answer is straightforward, though not simple: we are waiting for God's kingdom, for the glimmers of light that mark Jesus' presence in our midst, for the fragments of end-times peace breaking upon us. In our waiting we are called to pray for the coming of God's kingdom, to announce Jesus' presence in our midst, and to seek to bring about more and more moments of end-times peace in our world now. We are waiting, but such a task of waiting cannot by any stretch of the imagination be classified as passive.

■

THREE

WAITING BETWEEN THE TIMES

John the Baptist

INTRODUCTION

I've always found John the Baptist, the focus of the third candle on the Advent wreath, to be a poignant character; for me, one of the most poignant in the Gospels. John is such an essential figure in the story of Jesus: he proclaims Jesus' coming, points people to Jesus, waits eagerly for him, and yet stands permanently on the outside. His role appears to be simply one of herald, announcing Jesus, pointing beyond himself, looking forward but never arriving. He stands Janus-like, with one face pointing backward to the old and another pointing forward to the new.

In many ways he represents waiting. The haunting question, that we will explore further in this chapter, is whether he ever "arrives." Does he understand what he has proclaimed? Does he comprehend who Jesus really is? Does he, in fact, know that he stands between the old and the new? He clearly discerns that God's kingdom is at hand, that something different is on its way, that Jesus is the one who will bring in this difference. But is that all, or does he gain a glimpse of a world transformed and made new in Jesus? On one level the answer is clearly no, since he died before Jesus' death and resurrection, but on another level the answer is maybe . . . he did encounter Jesus and may have gained an inkling of the life made new that he brings. In asking these questions, however, it becomes clear that these may be the wrong questions to ask. John was who he was and, more importantly, he was who he was called to be. He stood, waiting, between the old and the new, because that was what God called him to do and, perhaps, in that waiting he found meaning.

*But the angel said to him, "Do not be afraid,
Zechariah, for your prayer has been heard. Your
wife Elizabeth will bear you a son, and you will
name him John. You will have joy and gladness,
and many will rejoice at his birth, for he will be
great in the sight of the Lord. He must never drink
wine or strong drink; even before his birth he will
be filled with the Holy Spirit. He will turn many of
the people of Israel to the Lord their God. With the
spirit and power of Elijah he will go before him,
to turn the hearts of parents to their children, and
the disobedient to the wisdom of the righteous, to
make ready a people prepared for the Lord."*

LUKE 1:13–17

FOR FURTHER READING
Luke 1:5–23

The very first scene in Luke's story, after the
preface, sounds remarkably familiar. Haven't we been
here before? Luke opens with the story of an old man with
a barren, and equally old, wife who have yearned for a
child but have not been given one. The way in which Luke
tells the story indicates that he is reminded of the story of
Abraham and Sarah and expects us to remember it too.

The birth of Isaac, however, is not the only birth that hovers behind this story: it is also reminiscent both of the births of Samuel and of Samson. Just like Abraham and Sarah, both Manoah and his unnamed wife, and Elkanah and Hannah were unable to have children together, but each of them also has an additional characteristic that ties them to this story. While the extreme age of Zechariah and Elizabeth evokes the birth of Isaac, it is the promise about what John is to do that is reminiscent of Samson. When Samson's birth was foretold, the angel said: "Although you are barren, having borne no children, you shall conceive and bear a son. Now be careful not to drink wine or strong drink, or to eat anything unclean, for you shall conceive and bear a son. No razor is to come on his head, for the boy shall be a nazirite to God from birth. It is he who shall begin to deliver Israel from the hand of the Philistines" (Judges 13:3–5). The implication of the promise to Zechariah is that John, like Samson, was to take a nazirite vow, though another strong connection between them is probably their wild unpredictability. The connection with the birth of Samuel, more straightforwardly, is that the promise of their birth was given in the temple (1 Samuel 1).

The resonances with all these stories remind us to look beyond the obvious to understand the meaning of John's birth. The promises of the births of Isaac, Samson, and Samuel to couples desperate for children, were not so much about their having a child as about what the child was to be and do.

- Isaac's birth brought about a partial fulfillment of God's promise that Abraham would be the father of a great nation, that he would live in the land that God would show him, and that God would bless him (Genesis 12:1–2).

- The purpose of Samson's birth was to "begin to deliver Israel from the hand of the Philistines" (Judges 13:5). Samson's calling, that he fulfilled with varying amounts of success, was to fight against the powerful armies of the Philistines and to drive them out of the land.

- The purpose of Samuel's birth only becomes clear when he is called by God in the temple; here Samuel is charged to tell Eli that he and his family are corrupt and that God is going to sweep them away and set up something new and more faithful to God.

These three characters, then, stand behind John the Baptist: Isaac, the fulfiller of God's promise, Samson, a maverick fighter against foreign political forces, and Samuel, a prophet called to cleanse the worship of Israel and to anoint kings. John is to be a new Isaac, new Samson, and new Samuel. He is to fulfill God's promise to the people who, though now numerous and settled in the land, are alienated from God; as a maverick voice in the wilderness, he is to resist the political forces of his day, and as a prophet he is to challenge the worship of Israel and to anoint for them a new king.

As if that wasn't enough, this promise to Zechariah also proclaims that this new Isaac, new Samson, and new Samuel, will also be a new Elijah, who will prepare the people for the Lord (1:17, resonances of Isaiah 40:3 picked up again when John appears on the scene as an adult).

The promise to Zechariah makes clear that John is to be the distillation of Jewish hope: a figure of judgment and promise; of condemnation and hope. He is to stand in a long, long line of those called to draw people back to God. John the Baptist is to be the newest of old characters from the Hebrew Scriptures of the Old Testament bringing fulfillment, judgment, and a new start, but he is also to be the oldest of new characters in Jesus' ministry preparing people for the one who is to come. He looks backward and forward, forming a link between old and new.

In some ways John is the epitome of Advent: a figure in whom the past and the future meet in an explosive message for the present. John may be called to waiting, but his waiting can hardly be called passive; John's is an abrasive, disruptive, unsettling waiting—a waiting that is about as active as it is possible to be.

Fear came over all their neighbors,
and all these things were talked about
throughout the entire hill country of Judea.
All who heard them pondered them and said,
"What then will this child become?"
For, indeed, the hand of the Lord was with him.

LUKE 1 : 6 5 – 6 6

FOR FURTHER READING
Luke 1:59–66

You can almost hear the gossip that spread like wild-
fire through the hill country of Judea: "Have you heard
about Zechariah? You know Zechariah the priest! Saw an
angel in the temple, so they say. Anyway he can't speak
now, or at least he couldn't until his son was born, *then*
he finds his voice and you'll never guess what he said! Oh
you've heard already . . . never mind, but your neighbor
might not have. . . . Have you heard about Zechariah?"

The events surrounding John's birth really must have
caused a stir. It is not every day that a priest in the temple
has a vision of an angel, is struck dumb, has a son by an
elderly, barren wife, and recovers his voice in the nick
of time to overturn what the boy was to be called and
announce his God-given name. It really would be a story

worthy of the best gossips in the region, but as verse 65 makes clear, the effect of these events is a feast not just of gossip but also of fear. The question is what caused this fear? This fear is probably the same kind of fear that we noticed in Chapter 1 (pp. 23–24): appropriate, awesome fear inspired by an encounter with the true, but dangerous, God.

What is interesting is that we might expect Zechariah to be afraid, as indeed he was—in verse 12 the text tells us that he wasn't just afraid he was terrified/upset/disturbed *and* had fear fall on him. But why would the people living in the hill country be afraid? The answer is quite straightforward: the events of John's birth mark him out as being chosen by God. The people of the Judean hill country know enough to realize that this means that God will be summoning him to something special in which, due to their proximity to him, they will almost certainly be caught up. The lives of Zechariah and Elizabeth are not the only ones that will be turned upside down by this divine intervention; fear is probably an appropriate response to this news.

One of the intriguing features of this story is the kerfuffle over the choosing of John's name. There are a couple of odd details here:

- The insistence on calling John after his father. It was much more common to name a child after their grandfather than after their father. The best explanation offered for this happening is that the circumstances of Zechariah's dumbness meant that, symbolically, the people saw John as needing to follow in his father's footsteps straightaway.

- That John should be named at his circumcision (eight days after his birth). The practice in the Hebrew Bible was to name people at their birth, not at their circumcision (as Abraham did with the naming of Isaac in Genesis 21:3). The practice of naming people at their circumcision only grew up in later Judaism long after John's birth. This is not a hugely important detail and probably exists so that Luke can draw additional attention to the importance of the name.

The name John is significant here and the odd details serve to focus our attention on it. The name is based on a subtle play on words. The Hebrew name "Yohanan" (John) comes from the phrase "God has shown favor"; the second half of the name (*hanan*) is connected to the Hebrew word *tehinna*, that means "prayer for favor." In Greek, *tehinna* is normally translated as *deesis*, the word used by the angel to Zechariah in 1:13 when he says, "Your *prayer* has been heard." John's name then is a symbolic prophecy about God's fulfillment of Zechariah's prayer: Zechariah's insistence on calling his son "God has shown favor," or John, is a sign that now, at last, he can recognize the truth of the fulfillment of God's promise: now Zechariah is ready to proclaim John's birth for what it is—he can speak again.

The news of John's birth is big enough to encourage people to wonder about what kind of person he would be. It is remarkable how much people manage to read into a baby's personality about what they are going to be when they grow up: a baby who kicks hard in the womb will be a footballer; a baby who is born early will always be in a hurry, and conversely, one born late will be late for ever. A baby who sleeps a lot will be laid back as an adult; one who cries a lot will be a handful. Could they have guessed from John's unorthodox conception, his father's miraculous dumbness, and the unusual way in which he was named that he was to become an unpredictable, wild, prophetic character, living in the desert, eating locusts and wild honey, and upsetting the rulers of the land?

It is highly unlikely that they could have guessed even a fraction of this, because the events of John's birth simply indicate that John was chosen by God. Part of the adventure of following God is discovering where God will lead us next. Knowing *that* God has called us tells us nothing about *what* God has called us to. Even those who are more or less comfortably established in doing something to which they have been called by God cannot be certain that tomorrow, next month, or next year this calling will remain the same. The people who heard about John's birth knew that God was calling him and pondered where that calling might lead. They knew enough, however, to know that this kind of calling had consequences for all who were caught in its wake; it is hardly surprising that they were afraid.

John the baptizer appeared in the wilderness, proclaiming a baptism of repentance for the forgiveness of sins. And people from the whole Judean countryside and all the people of Jerusalem were going out to him, and were baptized by him in the river Jordan, confessing their sins.

MARK 1:4-5

FOR FURTHER READING
Mark 1:2–11

In Mark's Gospel John the Baptist bursts onto the scene. Those who have read Luke's account of John's conception and birth, as we have done above, have already been pointed in the direction of pondering what this baby might become; in Luke's Gospel John's arrival, in the midst of our pondering, is much more gentle. In Mark, however, there is scarcely time to draw breath between discovering that this is the "beginning of the good news of Jesus Christ, the Son of God," and the eruption of this strange baptizer figure onto our pages. It seems that Mark is trying to tell us something about this figure: John is disruptive, exploding into the story, disturbing and unsettling people.

One of the reasons that we often overlook the significance of John is because we take his message for granted. We are so used to baptism, repentance, and the forgiveness of sins that his message is almost commonplace. It is hard for us to comprehend the radical nature of his message. We are told that John came proclaiming "repentance baptism into the forgiveness of sins" (that is a literal translation of the Greek); this could mean repentance *and* baptism for the forgiveness of sins or repentance-baptism for the forgiveness of sins (though we have no space to explore this here, there is an intriguing difference between the two that is worth thinking about).

While baptism itself was not new to John, John's particular version of it was. Ritual washing was common in first-century Judaism. Numerous *miqva'ot*, or baths for ritual immersion, have been found both in Jerusalem and in Qumran. Ritual washing was what one did, regularly, in preparation for worship. In contrast, John's baptism was a single, unrepeatable action. Some people have suggested that this baptism is closer to the one of immersion required of Gentiles when they became proselytes, that is, converted to Judaism, or of initiates into the Qumran community. This kind of washing symbolized a movement from one state into another and in particular was the means of an outsider moving to the status of insider.

Even if it is to be likened to this kind of initiates' baptism, John's baptism remains different. One of the most significant differences is that it is done by one person to another. All the familiar ritual cleansings in

Judaism were self-administered; John's baptism was done by him to someone else. This makes John's baptism a community event as opposed to personal cleansing. John's baptism, therefore, carries with it a corporate, community significance that stretches beyond an individual.

A second major difference is that John's baptism took place not in the specially built, ritually clean *miqva'ot*, but in the grubby, unappetizing river Jordan. Here true cleansing can take place, because it is a place of homecoming (see the story of Joshua's crossing the Jordan as they settled in the land in Joshua 3:1–17) and healing (see the story of the healing of Naaman, the Syrian commander, by Elisha in 2 Kings 5:1–27), but it is a cleansing of an entirely different kind.

Most unusually of all, the baptism of John was not a means of allowing outsiders to become insiders but for insiders (the people of Judea and Jerusalem) to repent. The Greek word *metanoia* means literally a change of mind or heart. The inhabitants of Judea and Jerusalem are to have a complete change of mind or heart, which they symbolize in baptism. Behind this Greek word hovers another Hebrew word, *shub*, that probably informs some of the meaning of *metanoia*. Literally, *shub* means to turn and face in the opposite direction, which is, of course, what repentance really means, turning away from one way of being and doing and facing in a new and better direction.

The only way that these people could be prepared for the one who was to come was through an entire reorientation of everything that they knew and believed. One of the first elements of the reorientation required of them was an acceptance that forgiveness of sins could take place outside of the temple—a concept that would have been surprising and shocking, since at this time many Jews believed that forgiveness of sins could only happen through sacrifice in the temple.

John's message really was a message of preparation for the Lord's coming. If the people of Judea and Jerusalem could begin to understand that they as insiders needed a cleansing that arose out of an entire reorientation of their lives, and to recognize not only sin, but that forgiveness for this sin could take place not just outside the temple but outside Jerusalem, then they would, indeed, be a people ready to greet Jesus.

John's apparently simple message—"baptism of repentance into forgiveness of sins"—was as disruptive as his arrival in Mark's Gospel. While many people accepted his baptism, it quickly becomes clear in Jesus' ministry that they had not understood the radical implications of John's message. We may not comprehend it any better today. It is easy to assume that because baptism is an unrepeatable event so repentance/reorientation is too. Once we have undergone baptism, we can breathe a sigh of relief and get on with our comfortable, insider lives once more. Jesus' teaching suggests otherwise: baptism initiates us into a life of repentance, of lifelong reorientation into the things of God. John proclaims a message of lifelong disruption. Baptism is a once only action but repentance/reorientation is not.

Advent is a season that challenges us to grasp again John's disruptive spirit of reorientation, since it is this spirit that prepares us fully to greet Jesus, the one for whom we wait.

There was a man sent from God, whose name was John. He came as a witness to testify to the light, so that all might believe through him. He himself was not the light, but he came to testify to the light.

JOHN 1:6–7

FOR FURTHER READING
John 1:1–13

There is an old superstition that goes, "three times a bridesmaid, never a bride." I remember a certain frisson of anxiety that passed over me when, before I was married, someone said this phrase to me on my third time of being a bridesmaid. Surely it isn't true? Is it? Well in my case, it turns out that it wasn't, but it points to a deep down fear of what happens when one is too often in the supporting role and never in the central role. We become "typecast," set in a certain way of being that will shape us for the rest of our lives.

The reference to John the Baptist in the prologue to the Fourth Gospel indulges in a certain amount of typecasting. John is the permanent equivalent of a bridesmaid or best man: his role is one of permanent witness. His sole purpose in coming is to point to someone else. Historically, this passage has probably been included in order to overturn devotion to John the Baptist. Acts 18:25 tells us of Apollos, who taught passionately about Jesus but who knew only the baptism of John, and in the Gospels we read of the disciples of John coming to Jesus to ask him a question (Matthew 9:14; Luke 7:18). It seems that John's followers found him such a powerful prophet that they were unwilling to follow anyone else; the prologue to John's Gospel attempts to overturn this devotion by reminding them that John was only the witness, the herald, the person who pointed to the light but not the light itself. John the Baptist was called to be the person who holds the advertising board pointing to an attraction, but never the attraction itself.

In our world in which personal status and success is so important, it is hard to get our heads around the concept of someone whose whole *raison d'être* is to point beyond themselves to someone else. John was sent by God simply to testify to someone else, to point ever beyond himself to the one who really was the Light of the World. One of the important features of the Fourth Gospel is this theme of witnessing. John bears witness here and elsewhere in the Gospel (for example, 1:15; 1:34; 3:28);

the woman at the well testifies to the Samaritans in her village (4:39); Jesus' works testify to him (5:36) as does God (5:37); Jesus bears witness against the world (7:7); the Spirit will come and testify (15:26); and, of course, the author of John's Gospel provides one long testimony in the form of the Gospel ("This is the disciple who is testifying to these things and has written them, and we know that his testimony is true," 21:24).

Given the importance of witnessing in John's Gospel it is worth noting that, apart from John the Baptist and the author of the Fourth Gospel, who form the bookends of witnessing in the Gospel (John the Baptist at the start and the evangelist at the end), there is only one other human witness to Jesus: the woman at the well (the others are his works, God, and the *paraclete* or spirit). Just as John the Baptist recognized the truth, bore witness to it so that people believed through him, so this woman did the same: we are told that many Samaritans from the village believed in Jesus as a result of her witness.

In the Fourth Gospel recognizing the truth, believing it, and witnessing to it stand at the heart of Jesus' ministry. John the Baptist stands at the beginning of a long chain of those who are to point to Jesus. This indicates that, rather than being amazed at his ability to accept a lifelong calling to be the "also ran," we need to recognize that John the Baptist's calling is, in fact, our own calling. Just as he is called to point beyond himself, to deflect attention ever onward to the one who is the Light of the

World, so we are called to do the same. John's ministry sets up a chain of which we are now a part. He pointed to the truth so that "all might believe through him"; once believing they, like the woman at the well, should pass on the message to others so that many might come to believe and pass it on themselves.

John the Baptist stands as an example to us of one who is prepared, in all humility, to recognize that he is not the center but the periphery; not the attraction but the signpost to the attraction; not the Light but the one who helps others to see the Light. Jesus' calling to us all is that we pick up the baton of John and become witnesses to the one who brings salvation to the world. This is only a part, but an important part, of the reorientation that we were reflecting on in the previous passage. John the Baptist's message of repentance involves a huge reorientation in which the center of our being becomes no longer ourselves but one who is much, much greater.

The waiting we do at Advent reminds us of the importance of taking up John's baton of witness and passing it on, and of reorientating ourselves outward from the center of our lives so there is room enough for Jesus in the core of our being.

The disciples of John reported all these things to him. So John summoned two of his disciples and sent them to the Lord to ask, "Are you the one who is to come, or are we to wait for another?"

LUKE 7:18–19

FOR FURTHER READING
Luke 7:18–23

In the media, people say that effective communication is about 93 percent dependent upon presentation and only 7 percent dependent on content, which is, when you think about it, a depressing thought. One of the challenges for New Testament interpretation is that we only have the 7 percent and none of the 93 percent. This causes all sorts of problems, one of which we encounter here. The problem we have is not knowing with what tone of voice John asked his question; this is made doubly complex by the fact that it was asked through two of his disciples. The tone of voice is masked behind layer after layer of word of mouth: from John to his disciples to Jesus to oral tradition to written sources. But the question remains important: did his voice go up at the end or down? Is he wondering, "Are you then the one? The one I've been prophesying about?" Or is he doubting, "Was

I wrong? I thought you were the one who is to come but now I'm not so sure."

The answer rests on whether John recognized Jesus when he baptized him. The author of the Fourth Gospel is confident that he did. In the Fourth Gospel, John saw Jesus passing by and announced, "Look, here is the Lamb of God" (John 1:29 and 36). Matthew seems to agree: he has John the Baptist try to prevent Jesus from being baptized on the grounds that Jesus should baptize him (Matthew 3:14), but the other Gospel writers are less clear. Mark and Luke have John's prophecy of Jesus (Mark 1:7–8; Luke 3:16) and Jesus' baptism (Mark 1:9–12; Luke 3:21–22) but do not draw a link between the two. We are left unsure about whether he actually knew that the Jesus whom he baptized was in fact "the one about whom he prophesied."

Given this, it is interesting that Luke's Gospel raises the question further here by having John wonder whether Jesus is in fact the one. In this context, John's question is either hopeful or despairing. If he had not yet drawn the connection between Jesus and his own prophecy, then this becomes a moment when John begins to put all the pieces together and understand something about who Jesus is. If he had drawn the connection, then this question is more disillusioned—"I pointed toward you as the one, but now you are not doing any of the things that I looked forward to."

Both the tone of voice and the knowledge of whether Luke thought that John knew who Jesus was before this question are lost to the mists of time, but this question remains hanging in the air. Whether it was a moment for John the Baptist in which the light went on or off, we are left with the picture of someone who is desperately trying to work out who this Jesus is. Jesus' answer is crucially important. The disciples are to tell John that the blind have received their sight, the lame walk, lepers are cleansed, deaf hear, the dead are raised, and the poor have good news brought to them (Luke 7:22). This points to the fulfillment of a mishmash of prophecies from the Hebrew Scriptures such as Isaiah 35:5–6 and 61:1, Hosea 6:1–2, Micah 4:6, and Zephaniah 3:19. An interesting, but not hugely important point, is that the only factor mentioned by Jesus but not prophesied in the Hebrew Scriptures is the cleansing of lepers. This list of remarkable events is to be repeated to John, so that he can make up his own mind, with the somewhat surprising rider that those who don't take offence at Jesus are blessed.

This beatitude is unusual since it functions more as a challenge than any of the other beatitudes that Jesus says, which seem more like statements (for example, "Blessed are the meek . . . ," Matthew 5:5), but it begs the question of whether John ends up as "blessed" or not. Does he, like the Jewish leaders, take offence at what Jesus says or does he find the true answer to his question, work out who Jesus is, and receive blessing? The fact that we do not know the answer to this reminds us of the fact that, however much the Gospels describe the events of Jesus' life and the people whom he meets, there are always further characters lurking in the background of the story—us. It is not ours to know whether John did, in fact, put all the pieces together and work out who Jesus really was, or even whether he worked out that Jesus was in fact the person about whom he had been prophesying. The people who concern us are not ancient, first-century characters but modern, twenty-first-century ones.

Jesus continues to throw down a similar challenge to us: look, the blind see, the deaf hear, the lame walk . . . put the pieces together and see where they get you. The challenge, however, goes further even than this, because we, of course, now know who Jesus was. Our challenge is to recognize him today. This is yet one more example of the way in which Advent-waiting can clear our vision, sharpen our insight, and enable us to see Jesus, the one who was, and is, and is to come, in our midst.

"I tell you, among those born of women no one is greater than John; yet the least in the kingdom of God is greater than he."

LUKE 7:28

FOR FURTHER READING
Luke 7:24–30

Poor John, he has sacrificed everything for the prophetic message that he was to bring: he lived in the wilderness, spent his days proclaiming the message and baptizing, has been arrested, and now is in prison awaiting an outcome that we know is beheading. He has done all of this and yet, when Jesus speaks about him, he appears to undermine his place in the kingdom. Was this not enough? Is he to be forever on the outside looking in, caught between times, between what has been and what is to come?

Despite everything we know about John, he remains to us an enigmatic figure. The Fourth Gospel has him say of Jesus: "He must increase, but I must decrease" (John 3:30), and he decreases so much that it is hard to evaluate anything about him. In some ways he is the forerunner of Jesus: he proclaimed his message with such clarity and fearlessness that he upset the leaders of his day, was arrested and killed for his message.

In other ways he was entirely different from Jesus. The Jewish leaders that he upset were not the temple officials (although his proclamation of forgiveness of sins may well have upset them) but Herod Antipas, one of the sons of Herod the Great and ethnarch, or ruler, of Galilee. John upset Antipas due to the criticism of his marriage. This criticism was entirely justified, and it is hard to imagine that he was the only one concerned by it. Herod Antipas had already been married but had put away his first wife in order to marry Herodias, the daughter of his half-brother Aristobulus, who herself was already married to another of Herod Antipas's half-brothers. This marriage contravened not just one Levitical prohibition about marriage, but a whole handful of them, so it must have caused general upset, but John is the only one we know about who was arrested for his criticism.

The first difference between John and Jesus, then, is that John upset Herod not the Romans or the temple officials; a second difference is that John's death was brought about by what he said, more than who he was and what he did. Perhaps most importantly of all, however, is that his death was just that, *his* death, not a salvific transformative event for the whole world. John was a forerunner of Jesus, but his death simply serves to highlight the vast difference between John's death and Jesus'.

What then are we to make of Jesus' saying about John here? The first feature to notice is that Jesus acknowledges

John's greatness: "among those born of women no one is greater than he." This is a striking, and somewhat surprising statement; Jesus himself has been born of a woman, so to give John a higher status is remarkable. Jesus seems to be saying that John has reached a pinnacle in the whole history of salvation. God's intervention in the events of the world has reached its climax with John, because John has truly and faithfully acted as the voice crying in the wilderness announcing God's return to the people.

This is important. In the verses preceding this verse, Jesus turned to the crowd and asked them what they expected to see when they went out into the wilderness: in verse 24, "A reed shaken by the wind?" or in verse 25, "Someone dressed in soft robes?" These two sit oddly next to each other until we recognize their significance. A reed shaken by the wind would be commonplace in the wilderness in which one would find lots of reeds shaken by the wind. Someone dressed in soft clothes, however, would be entirely out of place, and, as Jesus says, their place would be in a palace. So John was neither commonplace (in that there were lots like him) nor out of place: he was unique but exactly where he should be. This is because he was proclaiming the message that God most wanted proclaimed to the world: that the people should prepare themselves for God's presence among them. John fulfilled his calling, a calling that prepared for God's greatest ever intervention in the world and as such was "the greatest."

So why then is he least in the kingdom of God? Surely that is unjust? While it may appear to us to be unjust in the extreme, here we need to recognize that Jesus has turned his attention to the ethic of the kingdom and is simply saying what he says many times elsewhere in his teaching: that the kingdom of God works on a paradoxical, topsy-turvy ethic in which the greatest is least and the least greatest, the first last and the last first. John is indeed the greatest human being, because he has lived out his calling to the full, but this is no reason to venerate him because in the kingdom of God it is the outcasts and the prostitutes, those despised by society, that are greatest. John is not outside the kingdom, he is simply taking his proper place within it.

Jesus' upside-down kingdom ethic is one to which Christians have never quite reconciled themselves. It runs so much against the grain of human nature that we struggle to comprehend it. Even when we are able to get our heads around the concept that in the kingdom things are upside down, it is hard for our emotions to catch up. It seems so unjust, so against the order of things . . . unless, of course, it affects us and suddenly elevates us to a higher position within the kingdom.

It is a challenge with which we must never cease wrestling. This ethic runs throughout Jesus' teaching: without this ethic Jesus' teaching would be entirely different. Perhaps the greatest challenge of all is not to accept it emotionally but practically, and to organize our lives and Christian communities around it.

CLOSING REFLECTIONS

John the Baptist is a strange character whose calling to the proclamation of "preparation" shapes the whole of his life. His particular form of waiting can hardly be called passive; his waiting was disruptive, abrasive, and unsettling. So unsettling in fact that it brought about his own death, but it was essential for Jesus' ministry. This kind of edgy waiting brings a different quality to the waiting we have explored so far in this book. Abraham's waiting was shaped by issues of faithfulness and trust, prophetic waiting by an acceptance of the overlapping of time, but John's waiting is about transformation that actively prepares for the person or event for which one waits and so helps to bring it about.

We began this chapter reflecting upon the poignancy of John's ministry and asking how much he knew about his betweentimes role. At the end of the chapter we are not much clearer. The Gospel writers do not tell us much about John's own self-perception and understanding, but what has become clear is that John's betweentimes waiting, as a character like a new Isaac, new Samson, new Samuel, and new Elijah, was what prepared the ground for Jesus' life and ministry. In fact, John lived out the repentance/reorientation that he himself proclaimed. The repentance/reorientation called for by John requires moving ourselves out of the center of our lives so that there is room there for Jesus. John lived this out through his life and death and stands as a beacon to us, challenging us to do the same.

■

FOUR

A LIFETIME OF WAITING

Mary

INTRODUCTION

The last month of pregnancy is a time filled with a mass of emotions both positive and negative. The waiting is nearly over. The longed-for event is about to arrive. All the hopes and dreams that have built up over nine months are about to be fulfilled; but this is accompanied with the knowledge that the only way to achieve these dreams is through the pain and suffering of labor. The future is both known (a baby is about to be born) and unknown (what sex the baby will be and what she or he will be like). Excitement is tinged with fear, anxiety with hope. This mix of emotions can only be heightened in a culture where infant and maternal mortality rates are high. Mary, like many other mothers-to-be both then and now, must end her period of waiting facing her fear with courage and optimism.

It is appropriate, therefore, that, as Advent draws to a close, we spend the last week watching and waiting with Mary, the focus of the fourth candle on the Advent wreath, remembering not only the waiting that she did as she awaited Jesus' birth but the waiting that she had to do for the whole of his life, and beyond. No parent-to-be can properly comprehend before birth the lifetime of joy, anxiety, delight, guilt, pleasure, and fear that await her or him once the baby has been born. This is a maelstrom of emotion that grows stronger rather than weaker as the years go by. Mary's accepting "let it be with me according to your word" (Luke 1:38) brought with it so much more than she could have ever anticipated, but this shapes her waiting and our accompaniment with her in this last week of Advent.

"Greetings, favored one! The Lord is with you."
But she was much perplexed by his words and
pondered what sort of greeting this might be. . . .
Then Mary said, "Here am I, the servant of the
Lord; let it be with me according to your word."

LUKE 1:28–29 AND 38

FOR FURTHER READING
Luke 1:26–38

What would you have said in response to Gabriel's message that you were about to bear a child? My response would have included a lot more arguing than Mary's equivalent of "all right then" and almost certainly more than a few rude words. Perhaps the account has been pared down and between the "How can this be?" in verse 34 and the "Here am I" in verse 38, there was much shouting, crying, and outrage. It is hard to comprehend the devastation of a message like this. If Mary was betrothed to Joseph, but still unmarried, she was probably in her early teens. Pregnancy outside of marriage was regarded with horror in first-century Jewish society and, although it was unlikely that she would have been stoned, since stoning only occurred on the rarest of occasions, she would have become an outcast from society, and her reputation would have been in ruins.

So how could she say "let it be with me according to your word"? How could she bring herself to accept the angel's message with such equanimity? If we read the story more carefully, though, it appears that she did struggle with Gabriel's announcement, but earlier in their conversation. It is fascinating to notice that Mary appears much more perturbed when the angel first greets her than when she has learned the content of the message. After Gabriel's initial greeting, we are told in the NRSV that Mary was "perplexed" by the greeting and "pondered" what sort of greeting this might be; or in the NIV that she was greatly "troubled" and "wondered," or again in the New Jerusalem Bible that she was "deeply disturbed" and "asked herself" what sort of greeting this might be.

The NRSV translation has clearly downplayed Mary's emotion at this point, but even the other translations do not quite communicate the potential anxiety behind the words. The Greek word *dietarachthe* means "deeply agitated" and *dielogizeto* can have the feeling of "argued" as well as "pondered" or "wondered." We need to add this to the fact that *dielogizeto* is in the imperfect tense, which implies on going action. So Mary didn't just say "I wonder . . . never mind it's OK"; her state of wondering, pondering, and arguing went on for a while. Rather than a mild crinkle of the brow and small question mark above her head, Mary seems to have been taken aback, disturbed, unnerved, anxious, troubled (and other such emotions) by the appearance of Gabriel.

This raises the question of what upset her so much? The answer must be found somewhere in Gabriel's somewhat flowery greeting. The greeting had three elements to it:

- "Greetings" or "rejoice" (*chaire*)—this is a slightly odd word to use (there are more obvious ones to choose) but the verb brings with it the implication that Mary will be in receipt of special favor or privileges.

- "Favored one" or "beloved one"—this verb (*kecharitomene*) is in fact connected to the word "greetings" (*chaire*) and emphasizes again Mary's status as blessed by God.

- "The Lord is with you"—it is promise of the overwhelming and vibrant presence of God that indicates that Gabriel's message to Mary is going to be challenging. The dynamic power of God's presence will, inevitably, have a profound impact on Mary's life.

Gabriel's greeting is somewhat reminiscent of the ancient Chinese proverb "May you live in interesting times," that can be seen as either a curse or a blessing. In the same way, Gabriel's greeting can either be seen as good or bad. To be in receipt of God's favor, especially beloved and granted his presence, can only mean that Mary's life is about to be turned upside down. She is surely right and sensible to be disturbed by this greeting.

Various commentators have noticed that the language used here has connections with the calling of Gideon in Judges 6:11–13. There, as here, an angel appeared, promised that "The LORD is with you," and declared Gideon to be a mighty warrior. In other words, he was declared to *be* what he *would be* in the future. In the same way, an angel appeared to Mary, declared that the Lord was with her and that she was in receipt of divine favor—in other words, what she would be when Jesus was born. It is quite possible that Mary's distress at the greeting of the angel arose from the fact that she knew that this was a calling like that of Gideon and that this could only mean an overwhelming challenge.

The annunciation to Mary is not often understood as a calling so much as a declaration, but a closer examination of it reveals that this is exactly what it is. In the way that many judges and prophets were called in the Hebrew Scriptures of the Old Testament, so Mary is called here to a task of gargantuan proportions. Her initial fear gives way quickly to bewilderment ("How can this be?") and then acceptance ("Let it be to me according to your word"). Mary may not, at this point, grasp the world-changing, life-changing significance of her calling, but then few of us do when we say that first tentative yes to God's summoning. She would almost certainly, however, grasp the immediate significance of her own personal disgrace and exclusion from the community, and deserves our admiration for saying yes anyway.

What seems important about Mary's calling is that she understands that being favored by God is as much to be feared as embraced. It is truly wonderful to be beloved by God, but with this comes challenges beyond our imaginings. It seems to me that Mary has it the right way round: the message *that* God has chosen her is far more frightening than what he has chosen her for.

In those days Mary set out and went with haste to a Judean town in the hill country, where she entered the house of Zechariah and greeted Elizabeth. . . . And Mary said, "My soul magnifies the Lord, and my spirit rejoices in God my Savior."
LUKE 1:39–40 AND 46–47

FOR FURTHER READING
Luke 1:39–56

When Gabriel left her, Mary evidently needed to do something. A modern teenager would almost certainly have picked up her phone to send a text; a teenager of twenty years ago might have picked up the land line to speak; one of fifty years ago might have written a letter; but Mary chose the only form of communication open to her: she set out with haste to the hill country in Judea where her relatives Zechariah and Elizabeth lived. Why them? The answer must surely be that they, of all people, would understand the miraculous message that she had just received.

This meeting between Mary and Elizabeth allows Luke to bring together these two, so far separate, strands of stories about miraculous conceptions. Both John and Jesus are conceived in impossible circumstances: the one because his mother is too old and barren and the other because his mother is too young and a virgin. One child has been yearned for, for years; the other not even thought about once. For one woman, conception is a blessing, marking her reentry into a society that had despised her for her lack of children; for the other, conception is far from a blessing and carries with it the potential for exclusion from society for having a child outside marriage. The gulf that exists between Mary and Elizabeth is bridged as in one moment of mutual recognition each one finds strength in the presence of the other.

There is a striking difference between Mary's response to Gabriel's message ("Let it be to me according to your word," verse 38) and her singing of her song of praise to God: "My soul magnifies the Lord. . . ." (verse 46). Despite Mary's stunning equanimity in accepting Gabriel's message that we explored above, her response is somewhat muted. You can almost hear the intake of breath, the gulp and the timid tone of voice, that said, in today's language, something like "OK then. . . ." How great a difference is Mary's song of praise, which bubbles out of her full of joy. So how did she get from one to the other, from brave acceptance to joyful praise?

The obvious answer is time. She slowly gets used to the idea and then is able to understand the profundity of what has happened to her, but, I suspect, something else has happened as well. First, she is now in the company of someone she knows and loves. It is when she feels at ease in safe company that her initial brave compliance can blossom into praise. Second, and equally importantly, she is now with someone who understands her experience on a personal level. As we noticed above, Elizabeth's conception, though in very different circumstances, was equally miraculous. When Elizabeth's baby jumped in her womb in recognition of Mary, Elizabeth exclaimed a blessing on Mary that ends with the words in verse 45, "blessed is she who believed that there would be a fulfillment of what was spoken to her by the Lord." Although this is primarily about Mary, it applies equally to Elizabeth and draws out the connection between their experiences.

Mary's song of praise, when it comes, is one of the most powerful in the Bible: the idea of reversal (the powerful being made low and the lowly being lifted up), the poetry, and the sheer joy of the song have made sure that it has remained one of the church's favorite expressions of praise for many centuries. It is widely accepted to contain a mixture of allusions to the Hebrew Scriptures.

Most noticeable of all is Hannah's song in 1 Samuel 2: "My heart exults in the LORD; my strength is exalted in my God" (2:1), and "The LORD makes poor and makes rich; he brings low, he also exalts. He raises up the poor from the dust; he lifts the needy from the ash heap, to make them sit with princes and inherit a seat of honor" (2:7–8). The connection here is made even more apparent by the fact that Hannah sang this song after she had left her longed-for son in the temple. But there are other connections too with the Psalms, in that Mary recalls God's past deeds, utters praise for God's action in the world, and slips between the singular ("My soul," "my spirit," in verse 46) and the collective ("He has helped his servant Israel," in verse 54).

This song draws on roots in the Hebrew tradition, showing how the God who has saved Israel in the past is acting to do so again. If we hadn't already realized what was going on in Jesus' miraculous conception, Mary's song now draws our attention to it: God, we are told, is fulfilling his promise to Abraham (with which we began this whole book) and helping Israel as he promised he would. Luke portrays Mary as the first poetic theologian of the New Testament: she sees the events of the world around her, makes connections between them, draws deeply on her religious roots, and pours this out in a beautiful hymn of praise.

This is a piece of theology that arises out of Mary's reflection on what the angel has spoken to her; out of her growing acceptance of its message; and out of a situation of love and mutual experience that gave space for her thoughts to flourish. Mary illustrates here the kind of results that can occur when we wait in the right frame of mind. Few of us can hope for results as beautiful and inspirational as Mary's song, but we are called, nevertheless, to put into words something of our relationship with God, and if we can't find our own words we could always use Mary's.

Then Simeon blessed them and said to his mother Mary, "This child is destined for the falling and the rising of many in Israel, and to be a sign that will be opposed so that the inner thoughts of many will be revealed—and a sword will pierce your own soul too."

LUKE 2:34–35

FOR FURTHER READING
Luke 2:21–38

We would be excused for thinking that "ponder" was one of Luke's favorite words: the NRSV has Mary do it after Gabriel greeted her ("and pondered what sort of greeting this might be," 1:29); the people of the Judean hill country do it after John's birth ("All who heard them pondered them and said," 1:66); and Mary does it again after the visit of the shepherds ("Mary treasured all these words and pondered them in her heart," 2:19). On closer examination, however, it turns out to be the favorite word of the NRSV translators, and not of Luke, because Luke uses a different Greek word for each one of these occurrences. Nevertheless, he portrays Mary as someone who thinks very deeply about what she sees and hears.

I wonder, then, what she made of Simeon's words to her. Christian tradition pays far more attention to the poetic *Nunc Dimittis* than to Simeon's rather more troubling saying here. If, as many people think, Simeon was a priest then this is probably a priestly blessing in line with that said by Eli to Hannah in the temple: "Then Eli would bless Elkanah and his wife, and say, 'May the LORD repay you with children by this woman for the gift that she made to the LORD'" (1 Samuel 2:20). If it is of the same kind, however, it is even odder than it first appears, since it isn't much of a blessing.

It is, however, quite like Isaiah 8:14–15 that reads: "He will become a sanctuary, a stone one strikes against; for both houses of Israel he will become a rock one stumbles over—a trap and a snare for the inhabitants of Jerusalem. And many among them shall stumble; they shall fall and be broken; they shall be snared and taken." Jesus, like God the Father in this prophecy, will become the means by which discernment takes place: some will stumble because of him and others rise.

Contrary to popular expectation the one who is to come will cause a division in Israel, between those who accept him and those who do not. He will be the means by which people's true natures are revealed: those who oppose him will reveal themselves to be who they truly are.

Simeon's blessing, then, is a blessing that speaks deep truth. We all know that a "nice" blessing that is untrue is of no value whatsoever. Simeon's blessing spoke the truth about who this child was to become, and as such becomes a much more powerful blessing than a more conventional blessing might have been. Unlike many others in Jesus' ministry, Simeon understands not only that Jesus is the one for whom they have been waiting for so long, but that he is not going to be as they expected him to be: his particular form of salvation brings with it division and discord because not everyone is able to accept it.

The remarkable thing about both Simeon and Anna, who appears a few verses later, is that in the daily crush of the temple, the comings and goings that made up the normal bustle of temple existence, they were able to notice the arrival of a tiny baby and to perceive who he was. These two symbolize the power of practiced, clear-sighted waiting; they alone of all these people in the temple discerned who the tiny baby before them really was and in their recognition broke out in songs of praise to God, as Mary did in the previous chapter.

We must end, however, with the final, and hardest part of Simeon's "blessing," which is directed entirely at Mary. Simeon's blessing is not just an abstract saying about the future of Jesus; it has practical consequences. This is the only place in the Gospels (with the possible exception of John's crucifixion scene) where the cost of Jesus' ministry for Mary is acknowledged: there is a cost involved in being someone who reveals what people are really like. The implication of Simeon's blessing is clear to us, who know the ending of the story. The consequence of Jesus' being a sign that will be opposed is death; those who oppose this sign will stop at nothing in their opposition and Mary will experience this as a sword piercing her soul.

Mary's waiting, therefore, is far from over. In pregnancy she had to face labor, that brought with it—guaranteed suffering, but Simeon's blessing indicates that her agony has only just begun. She must face the hardest waiting of all: waiting for pain. Abraham's waiting was for the fulfillment, however far off, of God's promise to him; Mary's waiting is of an entirely different kind and is the kind of waiting that requires deep inner strength. Simeon's blessing summons Mary to the kind of waiting that we all dread. We will never know whether she realized this at the time, or indeed, if she did, how she coped with it. Hard though it may be, Mary may well have learned profound lessons of waiting throughout her life: waiting for that which we most dread requires a depth and quality of waiting beyond all other types of waiting, but it is often in this kind of waiting that we discover the silent, brooding presence of God who lingers with us in our agony. It can be in this kind of waiting, from which we cannot escape so easily, that we discover that God has been present all along.

Then his mother and his brothers came; and standing outside, they sent to him and called him. A crowd was sitting around him; and they said to him, "Your mother and your brothers and sisters are outside, asking for you." And he replied, "Who are my mother and my brothers?" And looking at those who sat around him, he said, "Here are my mother and my brothers! Whoever does the will of God is my brother and sister and mother."

MARK 3:31-35

FOR FURTHER READING
Mark 3:19b–35

Many teenagers dream of the possibility that their family is not their real family and that one day their (almost invariably) rich, good looking, and (most importantly) unembarrassing true family will arrive on the scene to whisk them away to a bright and glorious future with a glamorous, prosperous, and harmonious family. Jesus is not indulging in a dream like this here; who could possibly imagine the disciples to be a glamorous, prosperous, and harmonious family? His saying is much more challenging than this and must surely be one of those piercings of the soul that Simeon foretold for Mary. Watching the Crucifixion was certainly the climax of Mary's "soul piercings," but it was not the only one: losing Jesus in the temple (Luke 2:46) and being rejected from the privileged place of being Jesus' especial family (Matthew 12:46–49; Mark 3:31–34; Luke 8:19–21) must both have brought pinpricks of pain, if not the full-blown piercing that Simeon foretold.

The events at the start of this story are unique to Mark, even though the rest of the story about Jesus redrawing the boundaries of his family can also be found in Matthew (12:48) and Luke (8:21), and they explain a little more of the circumstances surrounding this state-ment. Mark places this episode early in Jesus' life just after Jesus has chosen the twelve. At this point, an enor-mous crowd clustered together, to the extent that it wasn't even possible to eat any more, so Jesus' family "went out to restrain him, for people were saying 'He has gone out of his mind'" (Mark 3:21). Jesus then pointed out to the crowd that he couldn't be "Beelzebul, and by the ruler of the demons" since he was casting out demons, and then he said what he did about his family. If Mark is right about this context for the saying, then Mary and Jesus' brothers are being forced to understand a very difficult message here: Mary no longer understands her son better than anyone else; the Lukan story of Jesus' listening to the teachers in the temple (Luke 2:41–51) suggests that she may never have understood him.

One of the hardest things for a parent to accept— and one that all parents have to accept, though perhaps not quite to the extent that Mary had to—is that they do not understand their children: that there are facets of them that remain entirely unknown; experiences that the children will have that they will never comprehend. Parenthood is a long journey of leave-taking from birth to adulthood, though most parents do not have to let go of their children quite as completely as Mary was forced to do at the foot of the cross.

Jesus' saying here reminds us, as well as his mother, that he has family beyond human ties. Matthew's version of this story in 12:46–49 emphasizes this even more than Mark's version here, since Jesus speaks there of doing the will of "his Father in heaven." Human familial ties are broken in order to be remade into heavenly familial ties. Jesus will no longer do as his earthly family thinks fit; he will now act only as his heavenly Father thinks fit and is drawn into relationship with others who do the same. This does not cut off his earthly family so much as demand that they recognize that they can no longer dictate what he does or how he acts.

Jesus, in this story, is not wishing for a different family; it appears that it is his family who is doing this. They are the ones who are overwhelmed with embarrassment about what Jesus is doing and attempt to wrestle him into a more "acceptable" way of being. Despite Mary's incredible ability to comprehend and accept her calling from God, and to reflect on what it means in the powerful words of her song in Luke 1:46–55, she still does not grasp what this means about who Jesus is or what he must be. Social embarrassment still causes her to act just as we would, in an attempt to shush him, and make him fit in better. It is worth noting, however, that what we have encountered here is the Mary of two different Gospels. In Luke's Gospel Mary is the thoughtful ponderer of God's message; in Mark's Gospel, due to the lack of the birth narratives, this is the only place in which she appears. The differences may be less to do with Mary than with the Gospel writers's perception of her.

Nevertheless, the lesson remains: watching and waiting must involve the ability to accept that we can be wrong, that our comprehension is partial, and that, sometimes, people have to behave in ways that we think are misguided, if not a sign that they have gone out of their mind. This is not to say that we should hang around, watching life with an odd, impartial gaze, never intervening lest we be proved wrong, but that our waiting should be informed by lessons such as this one and our interventions made in a spirit of humility that accepts that we might need to revise our view at a later date.

Advent calls us, again, to a waiting that has its roots deep in a prayer and reflection that recognizes what we don't understand as well as what we do, and accepts that God, the one who waits with us, comprehends all things in ways that we will never grasp.

When Jesus saw his mother and the disciple whom he loved standing beside her, he said to his mother, "Woman, here is your son." Then he said to the disciple, "Here is your mother." And from that hour the disciple took her into his own home.

JOHN 19:26–27

FOR FURTHER READING
John 19:25b–30

In the previous two sections we have been encouraged to encounter the grief of Mary as at different points in her life she had to bid farewell to her son on his journey to the cross. One of the most heartbreaking things to observe is the grief of a parent as he or she mourns the death of a child. The Gospels never draw full attention to this grief, but it hangs in the background, suggesting a desolation that they never describe. The account of the women at the cross differs from Gospel to Gospel: in Matthew, Mark, and Luke's accounts the women who observe Jesus' death and later come to the tomb include Mary the mother of James and Joses (or Joseph); only in the Fourth Gospel do we find Mary, Jesus' own mother standing at the foot of the cross. Numerous attempts have been made to reconcile the accounts, but their content is so dissimilar that we must simply accept that they represent differing traditions.

The version in the Fourth Gospel contains the tradition that Jesus, at his death, establishes a bond between Mary and the beloved disciple, a bond as between a mother and a son. In order to understand this, we need to go back to the very start of the Fourth Gospel and the story of the wedding at Cana where, in this Gospel, we first meet the unnamed mother of Jesus (who remains unnamed throughout this Gospel). In this well-known and much-loved story, the wedding party runs out of wine, and Mary comes to tell Jesus of this, at which Jesus responds, literally: "Woman, what to me and to you?" (John 2:4). One of the challenges of this saying is to work out whether Jesus is being rude or respectful in his address toward his mother ("woman") and hostile, indifferent, or curious in his question ("What to me and to you?").

It helps, a little, to compare these two accounts. In the Fourth Gospel, Jesus speaks to his mother only twice and on both occasions he addresses her as "woman." The compassion of the second occasion, from the cross, suggests that the first occasion should not be taken as disrespectful, but much more important is the implicit connection between these two events. In response to his mother's statement in John 2:3, Jesus exclaims that his hour has not yet come; we next meet his mother again when his hour has come. Jesus' statement that his hour has not yet come is normally taken to mean that he cannot perform a sign before his hour has come; this seems illogical, however, because he performs other signs in the first half of the Fourth Gospel. The reappearance of his mother in the story when his hour *has* come suggests that it is his connection with his mother that cannot be fully acknowledged before his hour has come. Once his hour has come, then this connection can be fully acknowledged, treasured, and handed on.

The author of the Fourth Gospel's love of paradox is revealed one more time. Just as Jesus' glory can be only fully revealed at the moment of his death, in the same way the question asked in 2:4 ("What to me and to you?") is truly answered at the moment when the connection is severed; the depth of Jesus' relationship with his mother only becomes clear at the point at which it is handed on to the beloved disciple. There was indeed something "to me and to you" and this something (the relationship between mother and son, son and mother) is now established in a new relationship with the beloved disciple.

In the Fourth Gospel Jesus' death is a moment of glory when everything that is hidden is made clear. One of the striking features of the passion narrative in this Gospel is that Jesus is described as about to be handed over or actually was handed over by various people: by Judas (6:64, 71; 12:4; 13:2; 18:2, 5; 19:11) by the Jewish leaders (18:30, 35, 36) and by Pilate (19:16). Only at one point in the narrative does he become active and hand something over himself: at his moment of death John uses the exact same Greek word (*paradidimi*) to describe his giving up of his spirit ("When Jesus had received the wine, he said, 'It is finished.' Then he bowed his head and gave up [literally handed over] his spirit," 19:30). Jesus hands over his very essence at his death, but immediately before he does this he commends Mary to the beloved disciple and vice versa.

In the Fourth Gospel, then, Mary gains and loses all at the same moment: she gains a new son as she loses Jesus; she receives the recognition, for which we have waited since chapter 2, at the same time as Jesus is recognized for who he really is; Jesus is revealed to be truly her son when he is also clearly revealed as God's son. This kind of paradox, so beloved of the Fourth Gospel, affirms the irony alluded to by R.S. Thomas in his poem "Kneeling" that when God speaks something is lost—"the meaning is in the waiting."

One of the things that makes Advent so complex is the fact that it calls us to embrace the paradox of God's intervention in our world: that finding involves losing; that hiding involves revealing; that birth involves death, and so on. It is not for nothing that the Magi brought myrrh—spices used in burial—as a birth gift to Jesus and a permanent reminder of the paradoxical nature of his birth.

Advent beckons us into the nonsensical paradox of God in which deep truths can be found.

All these were constantly devoting themselves to prayer, together with certain women, including Mary the mother of Jesus, as well as his brothers.

ACTS 1:14

FOR FURTHER READING
Acts 1:12–26

We might sensibly expect that once Jesus has died, Mary's wait was over. Once that event, for which she had waited and feared throughout his whole life, had happened, she could go back to normal (whatever that would be) and live a life free of waiting. We might expect this, but we would be wrong. Mary only appears one other time in the New Testament and that is at the beginning of Acts. After Jesus' death, resurrection, and ascension, we gain one more glimpse of Mary. Acts tells us that after Jesus' ascension the disciples returned to Jerusalem and to the upstairs room where they were staying and, together with "certain women," of whom one was Mary the mother of Jesus, devoted themselves to prayer.

The best explanation of what was going on is that they were waiting because, as verse 4 says, that is what Jesus told them to do: "While staying with them, he ordered them not to leave Jerusalem, but to wait there for the promise of the Father." Mary, it appears, stayed with them while they waited, rather than returning to Nazareth (if she still lived there) or to the home of the beloved disciple. Our last glimpse of Mary, then, remains the same as that which we have seen throughout the Gospels. We see her, first, waiting for the fulfillment of God's promise of the birth of a baby; we see her, last, waiting for the fulfillment of God's promise of the Spirit.

I wonder whether she found this a familiar experience. It would be pleasing to discover that Mary's skills in waiting—for good: the birth of God; and bad: the death of her beloved son—had prepared her well for this final climactic act of waiting for God's Spirit, and that she sat in the midst of the disciples as they waited, teaching them what it means to wait and how to wait actively in God's presence for what will come. Much Christian artwork of this scene has Mary, just as I have described, right in the center of the disciples, but we will never know what role, if any, she played.

What we do know, however, is that waiting played a vital role at this stage of the story as it has done since the call of Abraham: the disciples needed to wait, together, for the coming of God's Spirit. Pentecost would have been very much less dramatic if the disciples and those waiting with them had scattered back to their homes rather than staying in the same room. It was this act of waiting together that allowed the experience of Pentecost to be as it was. Through waiting, the disciples and others accepted God's promise to them; in prayer they were ready and prepared for the moment when it came.

A less charitable reading of the situation might be that they simply didn't know what else to do: they were confused, at sea, and still anxious. The events of Jesus' death, resurrection, and ascension left them at such a loss that waiting and praying was all they could do. Even if their waiting arose from negative rather than positive motives—from their inability to decide what else to do rather than a full and glad acceptance of God's command to them—the result was the same. The coming of the Spirit at Pentecost was made possible because of their waiting and praying.

In common with so much of our Christian life, waiting laid the foundations for what was to come. Sometimes we are thrown back into waiting because we find ourselves unable to do anything else, but other times, particularly if we are practised in God-driven, active, expectant waiting, then waiting can flow out of who we are and what we do, and give God the space to intervene in the most surprising and world-changing ways.

We have no evidence at all of what Mary was doing with the disciples as they waited for God's Spirit at

Pentecost, but I cannot shake off the feeling that someone who had waited for as long as she had modeled for them the only thing they could do: godly active waiting. Advent is a time that summons us to embrace waiting as a way of life, to practise it, to hone our skills, and by doing so to lay down the foundations of a life shaped by waiting, so that when those times come in which we have no idea what to do, we fall back on that deep, still waiting in the present moment that opens up a space for God's intervention in our midst.

CLOSING REFLECTIONS

Mary is someone whose whole life was shaped by waiting. We find in her an example of someone who had no choice but to wait: from the moment of our first encounter with her she was called into the way of waiting for Jesus' birth, for him during his life, and most of all, for his death. Much of Mary's waiting was neither for something good promised by God nor for something long expected, as it has been for the other characters that we have looked at, but for something she dreaded most. This form of waiting brings a new depth to waiting so far explored.

I may be being tempted to make too much of her final appearance waiting with the disciples for Pentecost in Acts 1:14, but it seems to me that this was her first voluntary act of waiting. Jesus' life was now over. She was under no compulsion to wait for him any longer, and yet we find her doing it anyway. This choice at a time when, for the first time, she could have made an entirely different choice gives us the merest hint that Mary had learned a profound lesson about waiting during her lifetime so that she continued to do it even when she didn't have to.

Mary is a character about whom we know a great deal and very little, all at the same time. We know that events of enormous impact affected and shaped her life, but we do not know what she made of them. How she related to these events remains unknown. We know that for a large portion of her life she was forced to wait but, again, we do not know how she coped with this. Was she someone who found depth and comprehension in her waiting, or irritation and frustration? Did the waiting enable her to see more clearly or less so? As so often with biblical characters, we are forced to accept how little we know or are going to know about them, so Mary is something of a mystery and will remain so. She stands, an often silent figure in the Gospels, waiting for Jesus' birth and death, in great joy as well as in great suffering, and symbolizes for us the agony as well as the glory of waiting.

EPILOGUE

Many Advent wreaths have a fifth and final white candle that is lit on Christmas Day and that symbolizes Jesus Christ, the one for whom Abraham and Sarah, the prophets, John the Baptist, Mary, and indeed we, ourselves, have been waiting for so long. It is in Jesus Christ that we discover a perfect fulfillment of everything for which we have waited—as well as for those things for which we have not waited. Jesus brings both completion and surprise in our waiting, and points us forward to a lifelong waiting that can only find fulfillment in the end of all things. Perhaps most surprising of all, however, is the discovery that the one for whom we wait has been present all along; silently waiting with us in joy as well as in sorrow, in delight as well as in agony, drawing us further into the glorious paradox of God, who summons us to wait for that which has already happened and to remember that which is still to come.

It is this paradox that as the completion of our waiting draws near may cause us to pray, with R.S. Thomas:

Prompt me, God;
But not yet. When I speak,
Though it be you who speak
Through me, something is lost.
The meaning is in the waiting.

ABOUT PARACLETE PRESS

WHO WE ARE

PARACLETE PRESS is a publisher of books, recordings, and DVDs on Christian spirituality. Our publishing represents a full expression of Christian belief and practice—from Catholic to Evangelical, from Protestant to Orthodox.

We are the publishing arm of the Community of Jesus, an ecumenical monastic community in the Benedictine tradition. As such, we are uniquely positioned in the marketplace without connection to a large corporation and with informal relationships to many branches and denominations of faith.

WHAT WE ARE DOING

BOOKS | Paraclete publishes books that show the richness and depth of what it means to be Christian. Although Benedictine spirituality is at the heart of all that we do, we publish books that reflect the Christian experience across many cultures, time periods, and houses of worship. We publish books that nourish the vibrant life of the church and its people—books about spiritual practice, formation, history, ideas, and customs.

We have several different series, including the best-selling Paraclete Essentials and Paraclete Giants series of classic texts in contemporary English; Voices from the Monastery—men and women monastics writing about living a spiritual life today; award-winning poetry; best-selling gift books for children on the occasions of baptism and first communion; and the Active Prayer Series that brings creativity and liveliness to any life of prayer.

RECORDINGS | From Gregorian chant to contemporary American choral works, our music recordings celebrate sacred choral music through the centuries. Paraclete distributes the recordings of the internationally acclaimed choir Gloriæ Dei Cantores, praised for their "rapt and fathomless spiritual intensity" by *American Record Guide*, and the Gloriæ Dei Cantores Schola, which specializes in the study and performance of Gregorian chant. Paraclete is also the exclusive North American distributor of the recordings of the Monastic Choir of St. Peter's Abbey in Solesmes, France, long considered to be a leading authority on Gregorian chant.

VIDEOS | Our videos offer spiritual help, healing, and biblical guidance for life issues: grief and loss, marriage, forgiveness, anger management, facing death, and spiritual formation.

Learn more about us at our website: www.paracletepress.com, or call us toll-free at 1-800-451-5006

SCAN TO READ MORE

YOU MAY ALSO BE INTERESTED IN . . .

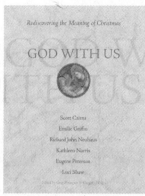

God With Us
Rediscovering the Meaning of Christmas
ISBN: 978-1-55725-541-9; $29.95
Hardcover with illustrations

Featuring daily meditations for the seasons of Advent, Christmas, and Epiphany, contributors Scott Cairns, Emilie Griffin, Richard John Neuhaus, Kathleen Norris, Eugene Peterson, and Luci Shaw offer a tapestry of reflection, Scripture, prayer, and history. Richly illustrated with classic and contemporary artwork, *God With Us* will make your journey to the stable in Bethlehem and the child in the manger utterly unforgettable.

Available from Paraclete Press
www.paracletepress.com • 1-800-451-5006

"In this winsome yet provocative Advent devotional . . . I began to sense something I had not understood before, in any of my other Advent observances—it is not just we who wait. God is waiting, too. 'The Lord wait[s], that He may be gracious unto you,' says Isaiah, one of the prophets who interests Paula Gooder most. God waits on us, for our attention, for our visits home; God waits for our vision and our ear."

LAUREN F. WINNER
from the Foreword

Is it worth the wait?

Paula Gooder shows how the spiritual practice of waiting is vital to our well-being. With warmth and insight, she helps us relearn the skill of waiting, and invites us to engage with real, flesh-and-blood people that are the subject of our Scripture readings and lessons each Advent: Abraham and Sarah, the Hebrew prophets, John the Baptist, and Mary. Each of them exemplified how to wait upon God for wisdom, joy, and the meaning of life.

PAULA GOODER is Canon Theologian of Birmingham Cathedral, is a visiting lecturer at King's College, and travels throughout North America and Europe leading workshops and inspiring Christians to deepen and express their faith in new ways.

LAUREN F. WINNER is the popular author of three books, including *Mudhouse* and *Girl Meets God*. She is Assistant Professor of Christian Spirituality a Divinity School.

PARACLETE PRESS
BREWSTER MA
WWW.PARACLETEPRESS.COM

COVER DESIGN: IHS DESIGNS

USA $15.99
ISBN: 978-1-55725-662-1
515

9 781557 256621